The Green Factor
in German Politics

Also of Interest

Europe and the Superpowers: Political, Economic, and Military Policies in the 1980s, edited by Steven Bethlen and Ivan Volgyes

Berlin Between Two Worlds, edited by Ronald A. Francisco and Richard L. Merritt

†*Contemporary Germany: Politics and Culture,* edited by Charles B. Burdick, Hans-Adolf Jacobsen, and Winfried Kudszus

The Basic Treaty and the Evolution of East-West German Relations, Ernest D. Plock, with a Foreword by Josef Joffe

Economic Relations with the Soviet Union: American and West German Perspectives, edited by Angela E. Stent

The Federal Republic of Germany and the United States: Changing Political, Social, and Economic Relations, James Cooney, Gordon Craig, Hans-Peter Schwarz, and Fritz Stern

Modern Germany: A Social, Cultural, and Political History, Henry M. Pachter

†Available in hardcover and paperback.

About the Book and Author

The Green Party evolved out of a number of protest movements of the late 1960s and 1970s and became a major political factor in the Federal Republic of Germany in 1983 when it drew enough votes to send twenty-seven members to the Bundestag. The author follows the party's rise from new social and ecological groups to its current place in the Federal parliament and provincial legislatures. He addresses the questions raised by Green Party members and by the unrest they have engendered—whether they believe in parliamentary democracy, what effect their policy of replacing delegates in parliament at midsession will have on the parliament and the party, and how they relate to Germany's traditional political parties. The answers to these and other questions form the background for an appraisal of the Green party in which the author traces the development of its role from a political irritant to a factor of serious influence.

Gerd Langguth is a political scientist and director of the Federal Center for Political Education in Bonn. He was a Christian Democratic party representative to the Bundestag from 1976 to 1980 and is the author of numerous books on German youth and protest movements.

Richard Straus, who translated the book from German, is a retired U.S. Foreign Service officer who has long been active in the development of German-American relations.

Gerd Langguth

Der grüne Faktor
Von der Bewegung zur Partei?

EDITION INTERFROM

CIP-Kurztitelaufnahme der Deutschen Bibliothek

Langguth, Gerd:
Der grüne Faktor—Von der Bewegung zur Partei/
Gerd Langguth.—Osnabrück: Fromm; Zürich: Interfrom, 1984.
(Texte + [und] Thesen; 169)
ISBN 3-7201-5169-7

Vertrieb für die Bundesrepublik Deutschland:
VERLAG A. FROMM, Osnabrück
Gestaltung: Zembsch' Werkstatt, München
Gesamtherstellung: Druckhaus Fromm GmbH, Osnabrück

The Green Factor in German Politics

From Protest Movement to Political Party

Gerd Langguth

Translated by Richard Straus

Westview Press / Boulder and London

Copyright © 1984 by Edition Interfrom

Published in 1986 in the United States of America by Westview Press, Inc.; Frederick A. Praeger, Publisher; 5500 Central Avenue, Boulder, Colorado 80301

Library of Congress Catalog Card Number: 85-40606
ISBN: 0-8133-0317-6
ISBN: 0-8133-0305-2 (pbk)

Printed and bound in the United States of America

The paper used in this publication meets the minimum requirements of the American National Standard for Permanence of Paper for Printed Library Materials Z39.48–1984.

10   9   8   7   6   5   4   3   2   1

CONTENTS

TABLES

FOREWORD

In the elections held in the Federal Republic of Germany on March 6, 1983, the Green Party received 2.2 million votes. With 5.6 percent of the total votes cast, the party was entitled to 27 representatives in the German Parliament (Bundestag). The election law of the Federal Republic, which provides for modified proportional representation, thus made it possible for the first time since the stabilization and consolidation of the German party system in the early 1950's for a protest party to be represented by exceeding the constitutionally mandated 5 percent of the votes cast.

By this time, interest in the Greens in the United States and in other Western countries had begun to stimulate inquiries and some concern. The Greens were already represented in the state legislatures of six of the eleven states, namely, in Baden-Württemberg, Berlin, Bremen, Hamburg, Hessen, and Lower Saxony. Fifteen months later, in the elections for the European parliament on June 17, 1984, they were to continue their success by polling 2 million votes or 8.9 percent of the votes cast, although voter participation was lower than in the Bundestag elections. They obtained seven seats in the European Parliament and joined ecologically oriented and extremist groups from other European countries in the European assembly's own "rainbow coalition."

No doubt the Greens in the Federal Republic of Germany and in other European countries have become a political factor.

The ability of the Greens by deliberate abstention to be instrumental in the formation of a minority government in Hessen is a significant example of their increased political influence, even if cooperation between the Greens and the Social Democratic Party governing in that state has at the moment been officially terminated. In a number of municipal councils, especially in cities with universities, the Greens are represented by more than 10 percent of the members. In the elections to the Berlin legislature on March 10, 1985, the Alternative List affiliated with the Greens obtained 10.6 percent of the votes cast, 3.4 percent more than than it had obtained in the elections four years earlier, on May 10, 1981. On the other hand, the elections held on the same day in the Saarland were a disaster for the Greens; they received only 2.5 percent of the votes, 0.4 percent less than in the 1980 elections in that state. It would be too early, however, to see these election results with an electorate of only 844,000 voters as a trend, particularly because special regional circumstances were a factor in this instance. In the May 12, 1985, elections in the state with the largest population, Northrhine-Westphalia, the Greens gained only 4.6 percent of the votes. This result shows that the apparently inescapable rise of the Greens has, at least temporarily, been slowed.

It would be wrong to overestimate the influence of the Greens on German politics or to dramatize it. A stable coalition of Christian Democrats (CDU/CSU) and liberal Free Democrats (FDP) governs in Bonn. The Greens have admittedly pushed the FDP out of several state legislatures by causing its voting strength to drop below the mandated 5 percent minimum; the resurgence of this party in the Saarland elections of March 1985 and in Berlin will require further analysis. All opinion polls confirm the stability of the federal coalition. The successes of the Greens, as will be shown, have been at the expense of the Social Democrats (SPD). Although the CDU/CSU received 48.8 percent of the votes in 1983 (as compared with 44.5 percent in 1980), the FDP received only 7 percent as compared to 10.6

percent in 1980. The losses sustained by the SPD were considerable. Whereas that party had received 42.9 percent of the votes in 1980, the returns in 1983 gave it only 38.2 percent. The Greens, on the other hand, increased their voter percentage from 1.5 percent in 1980 to 5.6 percent in 1983. The subsequent state legislature elections seem to indicate a potential Green voting strength of about 10 percent nationally.

Those not familiar with recent German events may wonder why the normal four-year legislative period of the German parliament was shortened in March 1983 for a parliament elected in October 1980. For the first time in the history of the Federal Republic of Germany a "constructive vote of no confidence" toppled Chancellor Helmut Schmidt on October 1, 1982, when the FDP switched from its previous partnership with the SPD to a new coalition with the Christian Union parties. The new coalition then decided to hold elections within six months. It pulled off a major victory in these elections on March 6, 1983. The question of NATO's rearmament—the implementation of the NATO dual decision of 1979 providing for the stationing of cruise and Pershing II missiles in Europe, including in the Federal Republic of Germany, should disarmament negotiations with the Soviet Union fail to bring about agreement by the end of 1983—played a major role in the election campaign. The new coalition favored the stationing of the missiles; portions of the SPD and the Greens opposed the rearmament plans.

The success of the Greens was no accident; it was the long-term result of the student protests of the late 1960s. In the second half of that decade, major student protests took place throughout Europe, especially in the Federal Republic. Their model was the American student protest movement, especially that centered at the University of California at Berkeley. Since those days of protest against authority—led at the time by the German Socialist Students Association (SDS)—a protest movement developed in the Federal Republic of Germany with many forms and with varying degrees of effectiveness. It encompassed the so-called new social movements, which included groups favoring citizen initiatives, ecological groups, organizations favoring alternative political structures, women's movements, squatters and, above all, the peace movements that developed in response to the decision to station Pershing II and cruise missiles in the Federal Republic. To represent these various protest movements in the legislatures and parliaments, a party arose that was viewed with suspicion by many of its own constituents because its participation in elections was seen as an acceptance of the very political and social order that the movement rejected.

How do the Greens envisage their political role and what ideas about democracy and parliamentary activity have they developed? Are they a party or a movement with diverse goals? Do the Greens, by their participation in elections, use parliament as a stage on which to propagate an antidemocratic ideology? And to what extent have the Greens developed their own professional politicians, even though they call themselves an antiparty party?

This book will try to answer these questions and will pay particular attention to the development of the Green Party and its policies since the March 1983 elections. My conclusion is that in the next regular elections, scheduled for 1987, the Greens will have a good chance to draw more than 5 percent of the votes and thereby remain in parliament. It must be assumed that their existence is assured for the immediate future.

An expression of appreciation is due the translator of this book, Richard Straus, whose knowledge of the political situation and whose intuitive understanding contributed to making this book on the green-ecological movement in the Federal Republic of Germany available to English-speaking readers.

Gerd Langguth
Bonn, June 1985

THE FORMATION OF THE GREEN PARTY

Early Ecological and Alternative Movements

It is not possible to understand the establishment of the Green Party as the parliamentary arm of a protest movement without at least a cursory examination of the history of protest movements in the Federal Republic of Germany. In the 1950's, a broadly based movement sought to prevent the establishment of German armed forces. During that period, the *ohne mich* (without me) movement sought to opt out of difficult political decisions. In 1955, moreover, a movement opposed Germany's new military alliances. These short-lived movements were followed in 1957 by a movement against nuclear warfare and in the early 1960's by Easter March antinuclear movements with origins in Great Britain. None of these movements had major popular appeal. Less political, even though directed against accepted values and morals were the counterculture movements of the 1950's and 1960's (such as the beatniks, hippies, and yippies) that also failed to achieve any real importance.

Not until the second half of the 1960's did a major protest movement develop in Western industrialized countries. It originated with students and was represented in the Federal Republic of Germany by the German Socialist Student Association (SDS).[1] Their protest against the so-called Establishment led to the development of a political ideology influenced primarily by

German-born Stanford University professor, Herbert Marcuse. Using the psychoanalytical theories of Sigmund Freud as a starting point, Marcuse sought to establish a "new human being" living in a "culture without suppression" and "without repressive mechanisms." The protest movement was also inspired by Prof. Max Horkheimer who, as a result of the events of World War II, had developed the theory of the authoritarian state. The antiauthority revolt of the SDS influenced large segments of the student population, resulting not only in a revolt against "outdated" university structures but also against what they viewed as the narrow-minded moral and value system of the German middle class. The protest movement found its central theme in its protests against the U.S. military involvement in Vietnam. The reasons for this movement's successful appeal among students were manifold; initially it found a surprised audience, unprepared for this type of protest movement. Such sociologists of the youth movement as Helmut Schelsky and Ludwig von Friedeburg were equally surprised; as late as the early 1960's Friedeburg had noted that students in this modern society "had ceased to be the ferment of productive unrest."[2]

The fertile soil for the youth movement's message was based in part on the increasing anonymity of modern society, where the loneliness of the individual often leads to a desire to associate with others for the sake of group interaction, and in part on the loss of appeal of traditional values. In the Federal Republic of Germany, the existence of a coalition that governed from 1966 to 1969 without any major opposition served to radicalize Left-leaning students, who were suddenly bereft of their traditional leftist opposition role in parliament. Prof. Richard Löwenthal of the Free University of Berlin saw the real causes of the protest as follows: "The militant attitude of young German intellectuals and their radical criticism of modern industrial society are developing within a clearly discernable socio-cultural pessimism. Their demand for the renewal of a radical utopia is based on a basic attitude of despair, their longing for a belief frequently based on nihilism which sees the humanistic values of our civilization as mere hypocrisy."[3] Another author emphasized that the source of the student movement required a sociopsychological rather than an economic explanation.[4]

The West German protests against authority began with the first actions at the Free University of Berlin in 1965 and reached their apex during the Easter disturbances following the assassination attempt on Rudi Dutschke, a protest leader, on April 11, 1968, and the campaign against the state of emergency laws in the summer of that year. Thereafter, the SDS appeared increasingly resigned to circumstances, and the organization dissolved itself on March 20, 1970. The first half of the 1970's was marked by the efforts of various political groupings to regain the influence among young people previously commanded by the SDS. The following political groups are worth noting:

- Dogmatic Marxist-Leninist groups, the so-called K-groups, Maoist-type Communist cadre groups that opposed each other vigorously. Some are still in existence, but they are now mostly without influence.
- Dogmatic Communist groups under the influence of the Soviet Union. These are primarily the German Communist Party (DKP) and its student and youth organizations: chiefly the Marxist Student Association (MSB), the Young Pioneers (JP), and the Socialist German Workers Youth (SDAJ).
- Terrorist groups. A few terrorist groups are based on the SDS tradition; many of their members come from the protest movement.[5]
- Antiauthority and anarchist groups and the Spontis. The effort to continue the antiauthority, anarchist, and largely voluntaristic traditions of the SDS never completely stopped. The Spontis (an anarchist group), in particular, were active in universities during the second half of the 1970's.
- Subcultures. Some of the protesters moved to a nonpolitical

level that favored a rejection of traditional society and embraced such ideologies as the drug culture and unconventional religious sects.

• Reformers. These former SDS members participated in the "long march through the institutions" predicted by Rudi Dutschke but then allowed themselves to become part of the political system they once rejected.

After the dissolution of the SDS, various groups competed against each other and obstructed each other's public effectiveness and as a result were unable to achieve any broad-based success. Not until the second half of the 1970's did the protest movement have a rebirth under the banner of environmental protection. This ecology-oriented movement attracted many political figures, among them Christian Democratic Union representative Herbert Gruhl, and many unknown adherents of the "Young Left." Gruhl's 1975 book *Ein Planet wird geplündert*[6] (The Plundering of the Planet) became a bestseller. He found that the race between the various ecological systems had become a race to the abyss: "It is a war blind with rage against the earth and the natural environment—and thereby against the fundamentals of human life itself." Gruhl drew the image of a balance of terror that led his followers to fear a catastrophe and doubt their belief in the inevitability of progress. These attitudes were engendered among all age groups—not only among young people. His criticism of modern civilization had been stated earlier in the 1972 Club of Rome publication *The Limits of Growth*. But it was primarily Gruhl's statements that united Germans pessimistic about society, rightists as well as leftists, in their rejection of existing environmental policies. The numerous citizen initiatives on environmental issues during this period indicate the great importance suddenly attached to them.

Parallel to this demand for a change in environmental policies, other indications of a "second" culture stemmed from the protest movement, particularly in the universities. This movement for an alternate life-style turned against pressures for achievement and careerism and drew upon traditions established by some of the reform movements of the turn of the century. Characteristic of the movement were demands for changes in personal life-styles, for a turn toward asceticism, for solidarity with neighbors, and for the careful use of energy and natural resources. The alternative culture was marked by such ventures as health stores, publishing houses for alternative literature, bars operated by and for members of the alternative culture and, of course, by rural and urban communes.[7] In the larger cities the communes developed into counterculture communities whose members not only worked together but frequently also lived together. Their homes, equipped with self-contained communications networks and governed by their own behavioral standards, often also served as substitutes for the family. A broad spectrum of alternative newspapers developed, growing in number from about 100 in 1976 to 240 in 1980.[8]

The search for an alternative life-style led in the second half of the 1970's to the so-called new social movements that attempted "at the edge of society, in its recesses and islands, to construct a model of a quiet, harmonious, ecologically balanced and democratic civilization."[9] The adherents of these movements considered themselves politically part of the Left, but they did not wish to identify with any existing socialist structure in which the trends similar to those in capitalist society were criticized. As a result they considered it an error, for instance, to be concerned solely with questions of property ownership. In these new social movements the primary emphasis was to change the everyday life of the individual and to develop a life-style critical of consumerism. In addition to anarchistic ideas, other elements critical of the existing culture, including those of Marxist origin and those based on existentialism, played a role in forming the movements' philosophies.[10]

The new social movements are without doubt an expression of the crisis of our times. Although concerns about protection of the environment link them to the ecological movement, the scope of their goals goes far beyond the environment. Large segments do not accept parliamentary democracy. The Spontis at the universities arose as an expression of a deep-seated longing for emotionalism, for an unrestricted expression of feelings. They attracted adherents because their philosophy gave expression to fears of the future and to a general search for utopia. But the movements also include autonomous groups that occasionally use force in demonstrations against the stationing of new U.S. missiles.

Although subcultural and countercultural tendencies existed in the 1950's, the broad appeal of the new social movements is a new phenomenon. They encompass women's movements, rural commune movements, pro–Third World groups, and many other types.[11] Basic opposition to technological progress appears common to most of them, and surveys show that these attitudes have spread, particularly among younger Germans. Asked if they saw technology as a blessing or a curse for humankind, 72 percent of those polled in 1966 saw it as a blessing. By 1976 this figure had fallen to 50 percent and in September 1981 to 30 percent.[12] Those fearing modern technology directly related this fear to its effects on health.

Phases in the Formation of the Green Party

The Green Party developed in five discernable phases. First, local citizen initiatives on the environment were formed, primarily in opposition to atomic power (beginning in 1973). [A citizen initiative is a group of citizens, or an effort by citizens united in a group to take a specific political action at the local level without reference to party activity.] In the second phase, consolidation took place at the state (*Land*) level, and voting groups and local parties were established, occasionally in competition with each other (beginning in late 1977). Third, the first nationwide consolidation was the group "Other Political

Associations—The Greens," which was formed prior to the elections to the European Parliament in 1979. Fourth, a federal party was founded in January 1980, and it first participated in federal elections in October 1980. Finally, the Greens became a party in parliament beginning on March 6, 1983.

Phase 1: Citizen Initiatives

The first indication of citizen initiatives can be traced to 1973. In 1975 such local initiatives sprang up throughout the Federal Republic; by 1977 nearly 1,000 such groups with over 300,000 members were affiliated with the Federal Association of Citizen Initiatives for the Protection of the Environment (BBU). In the mid-1970's between 15,000 and 20,000 citizen initiatives were estimated to be in existence.[13] Many were limited to local issues such as the prevention of highway construction. Nevertheless, the increased awareness of the need for environmental protection enabled these groups to reach a broad spectrum of the population.

Reaction to the construction of atomic power stations dominated this first phase. An example was the reaction to the plans of the government of Baden-Württemberg to construct an atomic power station at Wyhl. The plan engendered strong protests from local vintners, from opponents of atomic power, and from students at the nearby University of Freiburg. Regionally, the issue engendered cooperative action by German, Swiss, and French opposition groups. By June 1972, sixteen citizen initiative groups, primarily from Baden-Württemberg, founded the BBU and thereby created a coordinating office at the federal level. In some areas, the groups' reactions, such as that against a fast-breeder reactor in September 1974, led to demonstrations that drew as many as 10,000 participants. Such mass demonstrations were increasingly used by groups of the extreme Left to influence the citizen initiative and ecology movements, leading to a polarization between proponents and opponents of the use of force. Citizen initiatives on the environment continued beyond this early phase and moved beyond local or regional issues. In 1980, according to the Federal Office of Environmental Protection about 5 million citizens were active in the movement, organized in 11,328 regional and 130 multiregional groupings.[14]

Although some early citizen initiatives had a strong middle-class/conservative coloration and were directed against specific measures considered threatening to the environment, those that desired the creation of an alternative culture became increasingly dominant as time went on. They propounded an ideology that sought basic opposition to the existing societal structure. This trend was strengthened as collaboration from a broader geographic area became important. The views of these groups were soon reflected in the ecological platform of the BBU. Its program viewed "destruction of the environment, economic inequality, social injustice, and increased dependence of the individual on the authorities" not as avoidable side effects but as "essential characteristics of the system" and therefore as the proper objects of criticism.[15]

Phase 2: State-Level Organizations

Beginning in late 1977 clear trends developed toward the consolidation of citizen initiatives into parties or voter initiatives. On December 11, 1977, a party calling itself the Green List for the Protection of the Environment was founded in Lower Saxony as a state-level organization, and its members elected Carl Beddermann as their chairman.[16] In the election of June 4, 1978, this party obtained 3.9 percent of the votes cast. Beddermann had been the representative of the ecological wing of the citizen initiative movement. He and many of his colleagues saw politics as "the art of assuring the continued existence of humanity."[17] He was primarily critical of the euphoria about growth in modern industrial states but remained a supporter of the constitution and parliamentary democracy and an opponent of the use of force. From the outset, he differed with those elements that wanted to use the citizen initiative movement and the antiatomic power movement to further their own far-reaching political goals. Beddermann's position within the party became increasingly weaker; his resignation in September 1978 symbolized the decreased influence of the middle-class wing in the party, even though compromises enabled a coalition to keep the party in existence rather than to have various constituent groups compete against each other. In other states of the Federal Republic competing lists of "green" or "rainbow" groups did appear, especially in the city-states of Hamburg, Bremen, and Berlin where a large, active student population may have been the key factor. The word "rainbow" is used to indicate those groups of various colorations referred to in German as "bunt."

On January 29 and March 18, 1978, preelection conventions were held in Hamburg with BBU participation. The spectrum of participants reached from those desiring to protect nature, antiatomic power groups, and members of the the Communist Association (KB) to women's groups and gay rights associations.[18] The strength of the influence of the KB[19] in this "Rainbow List/Defend Yourself!"—as the new group was called—was described by one of its activists in an October 1978 publication in which he states that it "had been subsumed by the KB." It would be difficult to prove this allegation because KB members did not actively acknowledge their adherence to the KB and simply assumed a large part of the organizational activities that others were rarely prepared to carry out. Because of its hierarchial structure, it had great organizing advantages over the decentralized citizen initiatives.[20] The Rainbow List/Defend Yourself! also included members of the Maoist Communist Party of Germany (KPD).[21]

This Hamburg coalition was said to have had 150 member organizations. It is, therefore, no surprise that this rainbow movement, with its heterogeneity and antiparliamentary tendencies, was rejected by the bourgeois ecologists who proceeded to participate in the city elections of June 4, 1978, as Green List for the Protection of the Environment (GLU) but obtained only 1 percent of the vote. The Rainbow List/Defend Yourself! received 3.5 percent of the vote, among which were 18.2 percent of the ballots of the 18- to 24-year-old voters. That age group gave only 2.4 percent of their votes to the GLU.[22]

A second example of the dominant influence of rainbow-alternative tendencies is the Alternative List for Democracy and Environmental Protection, Berlin (AL). It was founded prior to the elections for that city-state's legislature on October 5, 1978, and initially had about 1,500 middle-class members. In the borough elections of March 18, 1979, it received 3.7 percent of the vote and sent a total of 10 delegates into four of the borough councils. At this point the AL had about 2,000 members, many of whom came from the formerly Maoist-oriented so-called K-Groups, especially from the KPD. Later activists also came from the less dogmatic Socialist Bureau (SB), from the Socialist Initiative, and from the Communist Association of West Germany (KBW).[23] About a quarter of the members and candidates had come from the KPD.[24] The trends toward this grouping were so strong in Berlin that a competing bourgeois ecological list could not be organized, in contrast to the situation in Hessen where three different groups existed in 1978.[25]

The situation in Schleswig-Holstein was different. A Green List was founded on May 21, 1978, which participated in the state legislature elections on April 29, 1979, but received only 2.4 percent of the votes. Members of a local association in North Friesland and an independent group provided its leadership. The best known leader was the "ecology farmer" Baldur Springmann who maintained that concurrent membership in neofascist organizations or in a K-Group was incompatible with the aims of the Green List; his position was adopted. This led to a split in the membership and the creation of a List for Democracy and Environmental Protection. The latter list, however, failed to participate in the state elections.

Any detailed analysis of this second phase demonstrates that the middle-class ecologists increasingly lost influence and had to assume a politically defensive role within the Green movement. Herbert Gruhl sought to oppose this development by founding the GAZ (Green Action for the Future) on July 12, 1978, as a nationwide organization. Within the Green movement as a whole, however, the GAZ was quickly branded as an organization seeking to impose solutions from above; as a result it remained solely a center for middle-class ecologists. At the time, Gruhl was still a member of the Bundestag but had left the Christian Democratic caucus. He was unable to obtain wide support within the Green movement even though the GAZ was later to play an important role in the process leading to the creation of the Green Party. Other efforts to create a federal-level party for the protection of the environment failed in 1978. Among these was an effort by the Action Association of Independent Germans (AUD) to become the political arm of the environmentalists, but its right-wing background prevented it from gaining adherents within the movement.[26]

Phase 3: First Nationwide Political Association

To participate in the elections for the European parliament scheduled for June 1979, the Green movement had to be constituted as a national political party. To meet this election law requirement, an organization called Other Political Associations (SPV)–The Greens (SPV–the Greens) was founded in Frankfurt on March 17–18, 1979. About 500 delegates participated in the founding convention. They represented the right-wing AUD, the GLU, the GAZ, and the Green group from Schleswig-Holstein. Another group—the Third Way—also participated; it was an anthroposophical group that had left its mark, particularly on the Green movement in Baden-Württemberg.

The top candidates of the new party were Petra Kelly, then an administrative counselor with the Economic and Social Committee of the European Community; Herbert Gruhl; Baldur Springmann of the Schleswig-Holstein Green movement; Georg Otto, the chairman of the Lower Saxony GLU; the author Carl

Amery and the artist Joseph Beuys who had been affiliated with the AUD.[27] The SPV–the Greens received 900,000 votes in these elections, or 3.2 percent of the total votes cast. Although no permanent party seemed to have been created on the federal level, the group maintained its Bonn offices and received about DM 4.75 million in campaign costs from the federal treasury—about 20 percent of the total campaign fund payments made available by the Bonn government to all the parties competing in the elections. A true consolidation of the various groups banded together to form the SPV seemed more and more likely.

Phase 4: Founding of the Federal Party in January 1980 and Participation in the October 1980 Elections

To formally create the Green Party, a convention was called at Karlsruhe on January 12–13, 1980. The total membership of the constituent groups throughout the Federal Republic, said to be about 10,000, was represented on a 1:10 ratio by 1,004 delegates. Two hundred and fifty-four additional "autonomous" delegates were allowed to attend, but none of these had the right to vote and only 30 were accorded observer status with the right to speak. The convention met immediately after the party's first election success: The Green List in Bremen had exceeded the required 5 percent minimum in the elections to the local legislature and had gained four seats in the parliament of that city-state.

The main controversy at the founding convention involved the issue of dual membership: Could a person belong to the Green Party and simultaneously to other competing political organizations? The faction around Herbert Gruhl opposed dual membership because it feared that various communist splinter groups could exert massive influence within the new party and in addition remain independent political organizations. Members of the rainbow alternatives and a large number of the "green" delegates favored dual membership, arguing that they stood for an "open party." After two days of tough debate, a compromise was reached authorizing the various *Land* associations to regulate the transition process.[28]

The rainbow and alternative groups were able to exert pressure on the convention because the bylaws of the original SPV–the Greens stipulated that a two-thirds majority was required to transform the SPV into the new Green Party and to give it access to the SPV campaign fund provided by the government. The necessary majority could not be obtained without a compromise on dual membership even though it obviously failed to resolve the underlying political dangers. Instead, it became the lever used to cause a large number of the middle-class ecologists to leave the party. Initially, Gruhl thought he could live with the compromise,[29] a view that the liberal weekly *Die Zeit* saw as a "prime example of the power of self-delusion."[30] A few months later, Gruhl was no longer a member of the party's board of directors. He initially stayed on in that body because the previously elected SPV board had continued in office and the platform adopted for the elections to the European parliament remained in effect.

The more important directions for the party's future program were established at its first platform convention in Saarbrücken on March 22–23, 1980. In the elections to the state legislature of Baden-Württemberg on March 16, the Greens received 5.3 percent of the vote and thereby sent its first representatives to a major state parliament. These Greens, however, acted with considerably greater moderation than their counterparts in other areas.[31] Although the election success was duly noted at Saarbrücken, the convention became a test of strength between the rainbow and alternative groups, on the one hand, and the conservationists led by Gruhl, on the other. Gruhl finally resigned from the board, basing his decision on the polarization of the party.[32]

The political differences between the two wings were brought to a head on the abortion issue. The conservatives urged that any decision on abortion should be left to each individual woman and spoke out in favor of the life of the unborn, whereas the rainbow and alternative groups wanted to eliminate all reference to abortion from the German penal code. A semantic compromise was found to bridge the obvious major difference. Other platform issues, such as "The Economy and the World of the Worker," "Marginal Social Groups," and "Women," also led to controversy. An alternative-oriented newspaper in Berlin, *die tageszeitung*, commented that

> anyone who might have expected that alternative party program goals might be adopted would be bitterly disappointed. The more than 600 resolutions and amendments submitted led to a voting mechanism which differed from similar conventions of the more traditional parties only by greater confusion but not by an alternative or more democratic decision-making process. . . . The resolutions to be voted on were solely a listing of all the demands which the Left, including its previously dogmatic and Marxist-Leninist factions, had developed over the last 10 years and propagated in public. They did not include goals related to the development of ecological principles.[33]

August Haussleiter, Petra Kelly, and Norbert Mann were elected to a joint chairmanship. A further party convention took place in Dortmund on June 21–22 to determine the participation of the Greens in the next Bundestag elections and to adopt an election platform. Only minor changes were made in the previous platform document. A draft plank on the relationship of ecology to the economy with which the Gruhl group took issue was deferred for decision by the party as a whole—the party base. On one hand, an effort was made to reintegrate the conservative wing by adjusting the Saarbrücken platform; on the other, greater limitations were placed on the influence of the GAZ under Gruhl. Haussleiter was forced to resign because of accusations concerning his activities during the Nazi period. The SPD paper *Vorwaerts* described him as a person who was "brown rather than green" and who had made his way from National Socialist surroundings into the alternative scene.[34] Gruhl became a candidate to replace Hausleiter. He was opposed by the Bavarian AUD chairman, Dieter Burgmann, and lost to him. Although Gruhl had accepted the Dortmund platform, he had, in contrast to Burgmann, not endorsed the entire party program. In the elections of October 4, 1980, the Greens received only 1.5 percent of the votes cast—a result perhaps influenced by the interest generated among the electorate by the clash between the two major party candidates, Helmut Schmidt and Franz-Josef Strauss.

Nevertheless, the Greens were encouraged by the election results in Berlin, Hamburg, Hessen, and Lower Saxony. In May 1981, they received 7.2 percent (9 seats) in Berlin; on June 6, 1982, they received 7.7 percent (9 seats) in Hamburg, and when new elections were called there on December 19, 1982, because the distribution of seats did not allow the formation of a coalition government, they received 6.8 percent (8 seats). They entered the legislature in Hessen with 8 percent (9 seats) and in Lower Saxony with 6.5 percent (11 seats). In five other states they failed to gain the required 5 percent of the total votes cast. At party conventions in Offenbach in 1981 and in Hagen in 1982, the major emphasis was on disarmament and unemployment. In Hagen on November 12–14, 1982, the alternative and rainbow elements were able to strengthen their role in the party at the expense of the ecologists. When Petra Kelly and Dieter Burgmann had to step down from their positions in the chairing triumverate because their nonrenewable terms had expired, Rainer Trampert was elected to the chairmanship. He belonged to a so-called Z-Group that had split away from the Communist Federation of Hamburg.

The 650 delegates at the Hagen convention, representing about 18,000 party members, spent a large amount of time debating economic issues. The issue of unemployment, particularly, became interesting when Rudolf Bahro, a former citizen of the German Democratic Republic (DDR), accused the economics committee of too close adherence to the program of the SPD.[35] Compared with previous conventions, the middle-class ecological groups were hardly represented. A new split developed between the group led by Bahro and Kelly, who rejected all attempts to cooperate with the SPD, and the reform ecologists who, though Marxist in approach, did not hesitate to remain in touch with other parties, especially the SPD. At the time of this convention, the budget of the federal association of Greens showed expenditures of DM 684,000, of which DM 270,000 was earmarked for personnel costs at federal headquarters.

Herbert Gruhl had left the Greens on January 19, 1981. The conservative ecologists with whom he was associated founded their own political party—Democratic Ecological Party (OeDP)—on October 11-12, 1981. At its first convention, Gruhl was elected chairman and Springmann his deputy. But the party leads a shadow existence. It received a mere 0.3 percent of the votes in the 1984 elections to the European parliament.

Phase 5: The Green Party in the Bundestag

On January 15-16, 1983, the Greens held a precampaign convention in Stuttgart-Sindelfingen during which a number of issues were resolved. Among these was the binding of representatives to party decisions, the rotation of representatives after two years, and the payment of the representatives. A platform was also adopted that was primarily concerned with economic and social questions and that documented the continued drift to the Left.

In the elections of March 6, 1983, the Greens gained 5.6 percent of the vote, and 27 representatives of the party entered the Bundestag. The next scheduled major elections were the June 17, 1984, elections to the European Parliament. A rank order list of possible representatives and a platform were prepared at a special party convention in Karlsruhe on March 3-4, 1984. This platform contained fundamental criticism of "the limited West European integration" and stated that "the starting point for integration had been the subordination of Western Europe to the global military and political strategy of the United States of America as expressed through NATO." In this platform the Greens also stated that they did not view the efforts of the traditional parties to bring about an enhancement of the authority of the European Parliament as a way to democratize the European Community but rather as an attempt to the develop the community further toward becoming a Western European superpower. In the view of the Greens, "current political decision-making structures" are totally unsuited to the solution of those European and international problems concerned with ecology and participatory democracy.

In the elections to the European Parliament, the Greens received over 2 million votes (8.2 percent of the total votes cast) and as a result sent seven members to that body. Voter participation, however, was only 56.8 percent, considerably less than the usual participation level in Bundestag elections. Contrary to the position taken by the traditional parties, the Greens stated that they would not only represent their domestic constituency but "the interests of all who are affected by the policies of the European Community but not represented in it."

The Greens chose the farmer Friedrich-Wilhelm Graefe zu Baringdorf as their caucus leader and bourgeois frontman in the European Parliament. For the second spot they chose Brigitte Heinrich, a native of Frankfurt, who had been active in the anarchist-terrorist scene in the 1970's and had been convicted of violation of the Weapons and Explosives Act and sentenced to 21 months' imprisonment.[36] The third and sixth delegates were two Berlin journalists writing for an extreme leftist journal, both of whom had been sentenced to 30 months of imprisonment for supporting terrorist organizations but are appealing their sentences.[37] All these delegates were to be rotated after 30 months of service. Similar groups in other European countries were able to elect delegates to the European Parliament and, as is the custom in that body, joined with the Greens into a single group of 20 delegates known as the Rainbow Faction.

Although the fifth phase of the party's development is thus marked by increasing participation in parliamentary bodies, it is also characterized by increased skepticism by a portion of the membership-at-large toward its representatives. The national party committee is clearly determined to strengthen its controlling role over the parliamentary representatives. Ex-General Gert Bastian's departure from the Bonn caucus in January 1984—which he blamed on its subversion by extremists—is another noteworthy event in this connection.

In July 1984, the differences about rotation became increasingly confrontational. The request by Petra Kelly to the Bavarian Green Party to exempt her from rotation[38] was voted down 120 to 80. Kelly appealed the decision to the party and the caucus but was unable to obtain the desired exemption from the party rules. Roland Vogt, whose base was in Rheinland-Pfalz, sought a similar exemption and after its denial requested that the membership-at-large be polled.[39] The question has some built-in explosive qualities because the departure of only two additional members from the parliamentary caucus would endanger the group's recognition as an independent faction and jeopardize numerous financial and parliamentary perquisites. Kelly declared that she would not leave the caucus but would not again be available as a candidate for office.[40] Joschka Fischer and others, who are also opposed to rotation, are apparently willing to accept the rotation edict in order to be available as candidates again at the next election in 1987.

The central issue of the seventh federal convention of the Greens held December 7–9, 1984, in Hamburg was the party's relationship to the SPD. The issue had been given impetus by immediately preceding events in Hessen. On November 19, 1984, the Green Party's caucus in the Hessen legislature had withdrawn its confidence in the SPD government under Minister President Holger Börner. Although the Greens had not been represented in that government, they had received numerous political concessions in return for permitting a minority government to rule, a situation that might be called a quasi coalition. The point of contention that had led to the temporary withdrawal of the alliance was the issuance of operating permits to two nuclear power plants in Hanau, Hessen. (By January 1985, however, the Greens again supported the passage of a budget by the Hessen government, thereby reestablishing the cooperative effort, even though it remained limited.)

Cooperation with the SPD became a major issue for discussion at the Hamburg convention, and a vehement debate led to a resolution stating that the Greens saw no current possibility of a coalition or support of a government at the federal level. There was no need to make such a decision now; any such step would have to be decided prior to the next federal elections and then be both an "expression of experiences and the result of a process of discussions at the grass roots level."[41] Formally, therefore, the question of a possible future toleration of an SPD government at the federal level, similar to the situation in Hessen, remains open. The Greens' Hamburg decision is an example of their effort to bring the maximum number of political views under one umbrella by vague and diffused formulations and to avoid placing any movements outside the party framework.

Elections to the Green's federal executive were also conducted. Of the three previous party speakers, only Trampert was reelected on the second ballot; he alone was able to develop a sufficient following. The others elected were Jutta Ditfurth and the former executive director of the Greens, Lucas Beckmann, who had held that position from 1979 to early 1984.

By spring 1985, two additional aspects of the party's history must be stressed: the elections to the state legislatures of Berlin and the Saarland on March 10, 1985, and the long-predicted rotation of nearly all Green representatives at midterm in the legislative session of the Bundestag elected in March 1983. The elections of March 10, 1985, ended in two widely differing results: a clear electoral victory in Berlin and a bitter defeat in the Saarland. The Green-affiliated Alternative List obtained 10.6 percent of the 1.5 million votes cast in Berlin and increased its representation in the legislature to 15 seats, as compared with the May 1981 election results when the Greens had received 7.2 percent of the votes and 9 seats. In the Saarland, on the other hand, they obtained only 2.5 percent of the votes as compared with 2.9 percent in the previous (1980) elections. The loss of votes in the Saarland became the first such loss in a regular state election. It is too early, however, to read any trend into these results. Both election returns led to intensive discussions within the Green Party about the extent of future cooperation with the SPD. In Berlin, the SPD's candidate, former Defense Minister Hans Apel, a member of the "right" wing of his party, had rigorously rejected any policy of coalition with the Greens and was defeated; the standard bearer of the SPD in the Saarland, Oskar Lafontaine, had in principle never excluded cooperation with the Greens and won by a landslide. For the Greens, the election results, therefore, require further internal discussion of the future relationship to the SPD. The elections in Northrhine-Westphalia on May 12, 1985, resulted in an especially painful defeat for the Greens. Although they were able to improve their share of the votes from 3.0 percent in 1980 to 4.6 percent, their failure to overcome the 5 percent representation hurdle signaled that the party must be prepared for future defeats at the polls.

The midterm rotation of the Green Bundestag members was an important turning point for the party. Nearly all Green representatives left the Bundestag during the weekend of March 30–31, 1985, and gave way to their successors. Petra Kelly refused rotation; others postponed relinquishing their seats for several months. The all-female caucus leadership resigned simultaneously. The newly elected speakers are Dr. Sabine Bard, a member from Bavaria who had chaired the Bundestag Committee on Research and Technology; Hannegret Hönes from

Baden-Württemberg, a journalist; and Christian Schmidt, a teacher from Hamburg. Eberhard Bueb of Bavaria, a successor, was elected to the post of parliamentary whip. These new leaders are virtually unknown to the general public. Dr. Bard is the only one of the six-member executive committee who has experience as a former member of parliament.

2

THE SOCIAL BACKGROUND
OF THE GREEN VOTERS

Factors Leading to the Creation of the Greens

In early summer 1980, a German research group estimated that the Greens could attract as many as 15 percent of the eligible voters.[42] Although this figure appears high for the period, polls among younger Germans clearly indicated that the Greens were increasingly becoming a political factor. Several causes, among them the following, led to the founding of the Greens as a protest party.

The Reduction of Social Controls. As did most Western societies, the Federal Republic of Germany experienced the development that the German political scientist Count von Krockow called "the dissolution of the milieu."[43] This was particularly true in Germany as an aftermath of World War II. In many ways, this social change was the result of the rapid changes taking place in society, economy, and technology. Where individuals had previously found a natural place in their own special milieus—rural or urban, middle class or labor—the extraordinary push toward modernity that took place in postwar society removed the protective function of the milieu and caused a loss of stability in many. As a substitute for the certainty previously provided, the new society, with its tendency toward anonymity for the individual, now developed alternative groupings and subcultures that provided care, certainty, security, and human warmth.

Changes in Values. Knowledgeable researchers noted a change in societal values, particularly in the younger generation.[44] This change was discernable in all highly industrialized societies and especially among the wealthier classes. Researchers noted a change in emphasis from material to nonmaterial interests, including a move to such goals as self-realization, increased leisure time, and happiness. As long as the material needs (social security, income, chance for promotion, and security of employment) were considered to be satisfactorily resolved, nonmaterial goals gained high priority, especially among the younger generation.

This change in values, recorded both by social scientists and in the polls, was also noticeable in the reduction of interest in the traditional search for achievement and career and the rise in personal, hedonistic interests. As a corollary, interest in the work place was increasingly viewed as of little purpose. The loss of importance attached to the traditional goals of achievement and career went hand in hand with a disdain for the willingness to take personal risks. Expectations that the government would provide total care increased. But the modern welfare state is faced with the paradox that the increasingly perfect social system it seeks to establish also creates an increased feeling of uncertainty and fear of the future. Changes in values are also noticeable in the expectations of education and in the relationship between the sexes.[45] Questions about the environment receive greater attention in this society and are part of the change in values. Large mass-appeal political parties are by their nature not in a position to respond to the nonmaterialistic needs of these "postmaterialists." The development of the Green Party is directly related to the role played by the two major German parties, viewed by younger voters as ideologically neutral and power hungry.[46] In spite of their commitment to basic values, these parties appear primarily as pragmatic—interested in gaining or retaining power—rather than as ideologically motivated. But young people are dissatisfied with this attitude since it does not respond to their search for ideals, for a transmission of values, and for a role in society.

Calcification of the Political Structures. In the Federal Republic of Germany, the political situation in the 1970's was marked by little change, a situation that the younger generation criticized as a calcification of the political structure; this attitude made a new political party all the more attractive. Although at the federal level the SPD-FDP coalition governed from 1969 to October 1982, the opposition Christian Union parties had participated in many of the government's decisions by their majority in the upper house (Bundesrat) and were therefore hardly in a position to absorb the fundamental opposition movement of the younger generation. Even though the Christian Democratic Union gained votes in nearly all state legislature elections, few policy changes seemed to result (except in Berlin and Lower Saxony, where special factors played a role). On the contrary, in the early years of this period, the SPD under the leadership of Willy Brandt had been able to absorb at least part of the protest potential of the student revolt of 1968. But the pragmatic policies of his successor, Helmut Schmidt, did not appeal to these groups. During the second half of the 1970's, the protesting minority found that it was no longer represented in parliament, not even in any important minority wing of one of the major parties. Only after the change of government in 1982 and the SPD's rejection of the NATO dual-track decision of 1979 did this party again seek an opening to the protest movement, in part to regain the loss of these potential voters.

Rise in the Level of Education. The general rise in the level of education of voters has resulted in reduced interest in the aims of their own social class and an increased identification with the political goals of a specific age group. This is a partial explanation for the rejection by a large number of young people of any ties to the traditional parties; it is especially true of those with formal higher education and financially comfortable homes.

Contributing German Factors

Some of the phenomena described occurred in all Western democratic and pluralistic societies. But certain specific German factors seem to favor the rise of the Green Party in the Federal Republic of Germany more than in other countries. The following must be included under this heading.

The Specific Historical Situation. Guilt for the outbreak of World War II and for the death of millions of human beings troubles the conscience of many Germans, including the younger generation. The natural patriotism in many other Western democracies is not equally well developed among young Germans; consider, for example, their troubled attitude toward national symbols. This low level of identification with the nation, which is also affected by the continued division of Germany, can lead to the dangers that result from an absence of personal self-awareness.

The Role of Ideology in German Politics. Traditionally, Germany has a large number of ideologically motivated political movements, such as the workers' movement, which in some cases draw on Marxist traditions. German voters are traditionally not decisively interested in specific political goals but have strong ties to political philosophies.

Proportional Representation. In countries with direct election systems, such as Great Britain and the United States, parties opposed to the political system have hardly any chance of defeating the candidates of the traditional parties. In these countries, those wishing to change the political system must infiltrate the existing parties and exercise their influence from within. In countries with proportional representation, such as the Federal Republic of Germany, political minorities are favored by the system, particularly since revenue support for election campaigns goes to new parties even when their voting strength lies far below the 5 percent limit required for representation. It is easier, therefore, to pass the 5 percent limit when proportional representation is available than to win in a single district on the basis of direct majority vote.

A Concentrated Appearance of Problems. Aside from the Netherlands, no country in Europe has as high a population density as the Federal Republic of Germany. Problems therefore arise in concentrated form and are intensively discussed by the mass media, especially television. In a vast country like the United States, there may be specific areas in which protest movements can develop without necessarily engendering a response from the population at large. In such countries, protest movements can run their course and disappear, particularly since such political movements appear to have less formal structure than in Germany.

Who Votes for the Greens?

The Green Party is represented not only in the Bundestag (since March 1983) and in the European Parliament (since June 1984) but also in six German state legislatures: Baden-Württemberg, Berlin, Bremen, Hamburg, Hessen, and Lower Saxony.[47] It is not yet represented in the remaining five states (see Table 1).

The party may be characterized as a protest party made up primarily of young people. According to the Federal Bureau of Statistics, 13.9 percent of the voters between 18 and 24 voted for the Greens in the 1983 Bundestag elections; indications are that an even higher percentage of this age group voted for the Greens in the elections to the state legislatures.[48] Even in the federal elections of 1980, when the total vote cast for the Greens amounted to only 1.5 percent, the 18- to 24-year age group favored the Greens by 4.8 percent. In the age group of 25 to 34, the Greens received 10.8 percent of the votes cast in the

TABLE 1
Voting Strength of the Greens in Various Legislatures

Election and Date	Name of Party	% of Vote	Seats
Bundestag			
Oct. 4, 1980	The Greens	1.5	—
Mar. 6, 1983	The Greens	5.6	27
	Eco-Democrats (OeDP)	—	—
European Parliament			
June 10, 1979	SPV–The Greens	3.2	—
June 17, 1984	The Greens	8.2	7
Baden-Württemberg			
Mar. 16, 1980	The Greens	5.3	6
Mar. 25, 1984	The Greens	8.0	9
Bavaria			
Oct. 15, 1978	AUD–The Greens	1.8	—
Oct. 10, 1982	The Greens	4.6	—
	OeDP	0.4	—
Berlin			
Mar. 18, 1979	Alternative List	3.7	—
May 10, 1981	AL	7.2	9
Mar. 10, 1985	AL	10.6	15
Bremen			
Oct. 7, 1979	Bremen Green List	5.1	4
	AL	1.4	—
Sept. 25, 1983	The Greens	5.4	5
	Bremen Green List	2.4	—
	Bremen AL	1.4	—
Hamburg			
June 4, 1978	Rainbow List	3.5	—
	GLU	1.0	—
June 6, 1982	GAL	7.7	9
Dec. 19, 1982	GAL	6.8	8
Hessen			
Oct. 8, 1978	Hessen Green List	1.1	—
	Green Action for the Future	0.9	—
Sept. 26, 1982	The Greens	8.0	9
Sept. 25, 1983	The Greens	5.9	7
Lower Saxony			
June 4, 1978	GLU	3.9	—
Mar. 21, 1982	The Greens	6.5	11

TABLE 1: *continued*

Election and Date	Name of Party	% of Vote	Seats
Northrhine-Westphalia			
May 11, 1980	The Greens	3.0	—
May 12, 1985	The Greens	4.6	—
Rhineland-Palatinate			
Mar. 3, 1983	The Greens	4.5	—
Saarland			
Apr. 27, 1980	The Greens	2.9	—
Mar. 10, 1985	The Greens	2.5	—
Schleswig-Holstein			
Apr. 29, 1979	Green List	2.4	—
Mar. 13, 1983	The Greens	3.6	—
	Democratic Green List	0.1	—

Note: See List of Organizations for full names of parties.

federal elections. One provision of the German election law assists the Greens in drawing this support: Each German voter has two votes, one for direct representation and one for the party of his choice. It is easily possible, therefore, for the German voter to send a representative from a traditional party to Bonn on the first ballot and to use his second vote as a protest voice and vote for the Greens. All of the Green Bundestag representatives were elected on the second ballot; they were unable to obtain a direct mandate in any district.

In the older age groups, the number of votes for the Greens drops sharply. In the 35–44 year group, only 4.4 percent voted Green, in the 45–60 year group only 2.4 percent, and among those over 60, only 1.2 percent. The Green Party is by far the most youthful. In the 1983 elections, 33.1 percent of its voters were under 24, 34.3 percent between 25 and 34, 15 percent between 35 and 44, 12 percent between 45 and 59, and 6 percent aged 60 and over. Nearly 70 percent of those who voted Green are therefore under 35.

The following data, unless otherwise noted, are based on polls conducted by the Social Science Research Institute of the Konrad

Adenauer Foundation[49] with field work done in cooperation with the Institute for Opinion Research. They represent the latest empirical data about the adherents of the Green Party throughout the Federal Republic. All those polled were older than 18; the polls taken in September 1980 included 6,206 respondents; in 1982, 2,015 respondents, and in March 1984, 3,000 respondents.

Men Versus Women. More men than women voted for the Greens—in 1983 52 to 48 percent. In the 1984 polls, the results were even more pronounced: 56 to 44 percent.

Single Versus Married. No party has such a large percentage of single voters as the Greens, a fact related to the youthfulness of its supporters. In 1980, 71 percent of the party's supporters were single; in 1984, 57 percent. The drop in the number of single voters may have resulted because many who had voted Green in 1980 had in the meantime married.

Religious Preferences. The Greens have more Protestant than Catholic voters: Fifty-one percent of the Green voters identified in 1984 were Protestant and 31 percent Catholic; 16 percent indicated no adherence to any organized religion. The last fact is particularly interesting and similar only to the 13 percent of the voters who voted for the Free Democratic Party (FDP). Both the SPD (7 percent) and the Christian Democrat/Christian Socialist Union parties (2 percent) registered fewer supporters among those who profess no adherence to organized religion. The assumption that the adherents of the Greens are especially "Christian" in their outlook is therefore without foundation; in fact church attendance figures show that 77 percent of the Green respondents indicated that they "never" attend church, 19 percent "seldom," and only 4 percent "frequently."[50] No other group of voters appears as removed from churches as the supporters of the Greens.

Urban Versus Rural. Forty-two percent of the Green voters live in large cities as compared with 29 percent of the total population. Midsized cities furnished 14 percent (11 percent of the population at large), small cities and towns 22 percent (28 percent), and villages 22 percent (31 percent).

Students Versus Gainfully Employed. Supporters of the Green Party are representative of 36 percent of the young people still being educated or in training, including military training. This group makes up only 9 percent of the total population. Housewives and pensioners, who make up 41 percent of the total population, furnish only 16 percent of the Green votes, whereas the gainfully employed represent 44 percent of the Green votes, a figure close to the national average of 48 percent.

Labor, Civil Servants, and White Collar Workers. Representation of the Greens in the ranks of labor rose from 8 percent in 1980 to 16 percent in 1984. Civil servants, on the other hand, decreased from 10 to 6 percent, independent professionals from 3 to 2 percent, and white collar workers stayed steady at 20 percent.

Levels of Education. The adherents to the Green Party are by far the most highly educated. In 1980, 51 percent of the Greens held at least a secondary school diploma; in 1984, 43 percent. This compares with 16 percent of the total population, with 13 percent for the CDU, 11 percent for the SPD, and 36 percent for the FDP.

Social Class. Seventy-one percent of the Green voters are members of the middle or upper class as compared with 64 percent of the total population. The representation of the laboring class among the Greens fell from 24 percent in 1980 to 19 percent in 1981 as the party found an increased number of adherents among the umemployed.

Summary

The sociostructural composition of the Green Party shows that it includes the better educated metropolitan population, frequently residing in cities with universities in which the counterculture was able to develop easily. Many of the party's adherents appear to have available spare time because they are students, unemployed, or single. A "psychogram" developed by a youth program sponsored by the German Shell Corporation in 1981 is of interest in this connection. This study analyzed the generation then in the 15- to 24-year-old age group. Even though this study is somewhat dated, its conclusions remain of interest. It showed that youthful Green voters received little psychological or material support from their parents and that they left the parental home at a relatively early age as part of their protest against the life-style and values of the adults in their home. They accepted the values of other young people and sought to postpone entering the adult world as long as possible, rejecting altogether the accepted main ingredients of adulthood. They tended to see the future pessimistically but sought active involvement in the present. They took their guidance directly from the protest culture of youth.[51]

According to this psychogram, the young adherents of the Greens differ sharply from the young Christian Democrats who received strong psychological and material support from their parents, adhered much more closely to adult values, and had close ties to their parents, which they loosen much later. They sought to take on adult status much earlier. They looked optimistically at the future, in regard both to their own role and to society as a whole. They also looked to the culture of commerce as a much stronger guide than the youth culture. Young Socialists, on the other hand, tended to have their parents' psychological support but relatively less material assistance; they left their parents' homes relatively early but generally not in protest. They tended to accept values from both adults and young people. They looked optimistically toward the future and accepted the offers of the commercial world as well as the guidance of the youth culture. They may be found midway between the Greens and the Christian Democrats.

Other data in this study provide additional information on the difference between young Green and young Christian Dem-

TABLE 2
The Expectations of Young People (percentages)

Future Events	Adherents of			
	CDU/CSU	SPD	Greens	No Party
The world will end through atomic war	32	44	76	49
Human beings will increase social contact	44	36	18	40
Technology and chemistry will destroy the world	19	24	52	28
Greater equality will exist	33	26	10	21
Computers will exercise total control	47	56	70	53
Wars will not be eliminated	60	68	79	63
Life will become closer to nature	46	37	32	39
Isolation will increase	53	54	76	62
Raw material shortages, economic crises, and hunger will develop	28	33	52	38
Society will not be worry free	60	62	84	63

Source: Shell of Germany's Youth Welfare Foundation (ed.), *Youth '81,* vol. 1, Hamburg 1981, p. 678.

Note: See List of Organizations for full names of parties.

ocratic voters. Eighty-five percent of the Greens, for instance, sympathize with the squatters; only 20 percent of the CDU youth do so. Seventy-six percent of the Greens believe the world will end in an atomic war; only 32 percent of the Christian Democrats hold this belief (see Tables 2 and 3).

The increasingly independent political position of the Greens also became clear in an Adenauer Foundation study in 1984. According to the results of this poll, 52 percent of the Green voters had previously voted Green, 20 percent had voted for the SPD, and only 5 percent for the CDU/CSU; 13 percent

TABLE 3
Adherents to Specific Life-Styles (percentages)

Question: Some groups of young people have become identified with particular styles—this is a list of such groups that have been in the news lately. What do you think of each group?

	I belong to this group/I live in this style	I do not belong to this group but approve of such people	I have no interest in this group but can tolerate it	I do not like this group	I oppose this group/They are my enemies	I have never heard of this group
Environmentalists	31	50	15	3	1	0
Alternative life-style groups	6	56	27	6	1	3
Nuclear energy opponents	20	33	25	16	5	1
Squatters	3	45	27	19	6	1

Source: Shell of Germany's Youth Welfare Foundation (ed.), Youth '81, vol. 1, Hamburg 1981, p. 488.

were first-time voters and 11 percent had previously abstained from voting. These data indicate that an impressive number of Green voters switched to the party by their own volition. The relatively large number of voters who came from the SPD confirms the fact that in the 1983 elections the traditional parties lost a significant segment of their adherents to the Greens, a factor with even greater numerical significance in 1980 when 36 percent of the Green voters had previously voted for the SPD.

Although 84 percent of the CDU voters support the program of their party and 75 percent of the SPD voters do so, only 65 percent of Green adherents say they favor the party program. This contrast may be traceable to the fact that the Green Party is made up of so many different elements that its supporters have individualistic attitudes. Moreover, their basic anti-institutional attitude prevents them from identifying with an organization increasingly in the process of becoming a regular political party. In an analysis of the motives for voting Green in the 1983 elections, 42 percent mentioned the party's support for protection of the environment; 23 percent, their dissatisfaction with the other parties; 22 percent, their identification with the goal of a "fundamental change in society"; and 12 percent, the party's strong support for the peace movement.

Two major groupings emerge from these data: the environmentalists and those dissatisfied with the existing political system. In Table 4 the differences in value orientation can be seen between the adherents of the Green Party and those of the other political parties. Green voters clearly pay less attention to law and order, reject the need for achievement in the work place, favor greater citizen participation in the decision-making process, and desire to live in a society that is "open to new ideas and intellectual change." Their responses in Table 5 show that they are more interested in postmaterial values than are the adherents of the traditional parties. Seventy-one percent see in the Federal Republic a society with too little tolerance, 68 percent with too

TABLE 4
Appreciation of Values

I would like to live in a society in which	Total Population (%)	Adherents (%)			
		CDU/CSU	SPD	FDP	Greens
Human beings are more important than money	51	46	55	47	69
Individual rights and the law are respected	50	59	47	51	19
Achievement can lead to personal satisfaction	30	36	25	34	16
Items of proven worth are valued and respected	25	29	21	24	6
Citizens participate in decision-making	25	18	32	18	45
There is an openness for new ideas and change	18	12	19	26	43

Source: Social Science Research Institute of the Konrad Adenauer Foundation, 8401.

Note: See List of Organizations for full names of parties.

little social justice, 67 percent with too little equality of opportunity, and so forth. In their view, German society overrates prosperity, industriousness, personal property, attention to duty, law and order, and so on. The figures in Table 6 are particularly divergent between the values esteemed by the Greens and those of the CDU/CSU. Table 6 presents data on the satisfaction rate with regard to the current political system; Table 7, the evaluation of *freedom* within the Federal Republic; Table 8, the confidence in federal institutions; and Table 9, the respective political priorities. The last shows that 90 percent of the Greens see environmental policies as the first priority, 84 percent so rate those related to the protection of peace. Security of the work place, a first priority in the other parties (see Table 9), ranks third for the Greens (of whom a large percentage are not gainfully employed).

TABLE 5
Value Structures

	Total Population		CDU/CSU Adherents		SPD Adherents		FDP Adherents		Greens Adherents	
	Correct	Difference (too much/ too little)	Correct	Difference (too much/ too little)	Correct	Difference (too much/ too little)	Correct	Difference (too much/ too little)	Correct	Difference (too much/ too little)
Friendship	50	−35	55	−32	51	−36	56	−38	33	−55
Industriousness	53	−2	55	−13	57	+5	54	−13	38	+46
Respect for marriage	39	−45	36	−55	43	−43	45	−47	42	−8
Leisure time	48	+23	49	+34	53	+15	42	+41	37	−22
Law and order	59	−13	62	−24	60	−9	59	−13	36	+21
Sense of duty	50	−15	49	−28	54	−8	53	−23	37	+28
Tenderness	44	−35	48	−30	44	−38	38	−35	23	−66
Well-being	38	+50	43	+47	36	+51	33	+61	22	+67
Personal freedom	68	−1	74	+7	69	−5	65	+4	42	−39
Care of aged	66	−21	69	−20	64	−25	69	−16	63	−14
Morale	40	−40	37	−51	45	−35	40	−44	34	+1
Political participation	59	−22	68	−12	55	−31	66	−17	33	−53

Degree of Realization of Values (percentages)

Personal property	62	+17	68	+14	61	+21	65	+10	43	+38
Social justice	47	−40	58	−27	39	−52	58	−26	27	−68
Equality of opportunity	47	−39	57	−25	40	−53	56	−25	26	−67
Self-realization	54	−12	59	−2	54	−19	52	+2	37	−40
Children	34	−57	37	−57	34	−57	27	−66	29	−63
Solidarity	47	−37	51	−32	45	−39	46	−39	27	−66
Equality of women	42	−30	47	−20	42	−39	38	−36	20	−60
Education	64	−7	66	−4	65	−10	68	−8	54	−22
Family	52	−39	50	−44	54	−37	52	−42	44	−33
Equality under law	53	−38	62	−29	47	−45	57	−37	34	−61
Service to general public	49	−38	51	−38	50	−38	42	−45	40	−41
Tolerance	46	−40	51	−35	45	−42	44	−44	23	−71
Responsibility to others	38	−52	40	−52	37	−54	29	−58	25	−65
Nationalistic awareness	47	−18	46	−32	49	−8	46	−29	45	+17

Source: Social Science Research Institute of the Konrad Adenauer Foundation, 8401.

Note: See List of Organizations for full names of parties.

TABLE 6

Degree of Satisfaction with Political System (percentages)

	Very Satisfied		More or Less Satisfied		Not Satisfied	
	1980	1984	1980	1984	1980	1984
Total population	15	32	84	61	2	6
CDU/CSU adherents	10	43	88	54	3	3
SPD adherents	21	28	79	66	1	6
FDP adherents	16	39	83	59	1	2
Green adherents	7	12	87	65	5	23

Source: 1980: Central Archives–Number 1053; 1984: Social Science Research Institute of Konrad Adenauer Foundation, 8401.

Note: See List of Organizations for full names of parties.

TABLE 7

Estimate of Freedom (percentages)

	Totally Free		More or Less Free		Not Free	
	1982	1984	1982	1984	1982	1984
Total population	49	39	47	53	5	7
CDU/CSU adherents	55	52	42	45	3	3
SPD adherents	49	34	47	56	4	7
FDP adherents	50	47	49	50	1	2
Green adherents	16	10	63	60	21	31

Source: Social Science Research Institute of the Konrad Adenauer Foundation, 8202, 8401.

Note: See List of Organizations for full names of parties.

TABLE 8
Confidence in Institutions (percentages)

	Parties		Government and Parliament		Courts		Police		Armed Forces	
	1980	1984	1980	1984	1980	1984	1980	1984	1980	1984
Total population	—	40	60	53	61	59	70	62	—	56
CDU/CSU adherents	—	53	34	69	62	67	71	73	—	69
SPD adherents	—	39	86	46	61	58	71	61	—	52
FDP adherents	—	35	73	59	65	62	65	61	—	57
Green adherents	—	18	32	23	44	30	34	32	—	20

Source: Social Science Research Institute of the Konrad Adenauer Foundation, 8401.

Note: See List of Organizations for full names of parties.

TABLE 9
Political Priorities in 1980, 1982, and 1984 (percentages)

	Total Population			CDU/CSU			SPD			FDP			Greens		
	80	82	84	80	82	84	80	82	84	80	82	84	80	82	84
Assurance of work	82	87	86	82	87	87	83	90	90	79	85	83	73	79	77
Limitation of air and water pollution	—	65	71	—	59	67	—	71	75	—	59	73	—	89	90
Greater efforts at peace	—	77	65	—	72	61	—	80	69	—	77	64	—	91	84
Price stability	74	72	60	77	75	62	72	76	62	68	63	56	55	42	40
Better protection against crime	60	68	50	67	74	56	56	66	49	53	58	49	33	39	24
Reduction of deficit	53	72	49	67	78	60	40	67	42	43	64	51	30	51	27
Continuation of policy of detente with Soviet Union	48	56	48	38	52	41	57	59	56	54	52	48	61	71	63

Limitation on number of foreign workers	38	46	32	43	51	37	35	44	31	26	38	23	16	17	13
Strengthening investment capacity of business	—	—	32	—	—	41	—	—	24	—	—	48	—	—	14
Increased savings by workers	—	—	25	—	—	20	—	—	31	—	—	19	—	—	31
Strengthening alliance with U.S.	41	—	17	52	—	24	32	—	13	31	—	18	14	—	3
Reduction of social expenditures by state	—	—	14	—	—	18	—	—	10	—	—	15	—	—	5
Increasing defense capability of the West	—	23	13	—	30	18	18	18	10	—	12	13	—	4	3

Source: Social Science Research Institute of the Konrad Adenauer Foundation, 8012, 8202, 8401.

Note: See List of Organizations for full names of parties.

3
PARTY AND CAUCUS STRUCTURE

The Organization of the Party

The seat of the Green Party is in Bonn; its highest policy-making body is the federal assembly that meets at least once each calendar year. In the period between meetings of the federal assembly, the federal party committee (BHA) meets at least quarterly and serves as the main policy-making body. Its decisions are binding on the party's federal board of directors. The latter is subject to the rotation system: Half of its membership must be newly elected each year. Only one reelection to the same position is possible; thereafter a member of the board is again eligible for election after sitting out one term. The treasurer is exempt from this rule. The bylaws stipulate maximum autonomy for local, county, and state assemblies in order to develop a decentralized party structure and participatory democracy within the party.

The Green Party has been able to finance its expenditures largely through the use of public funds. In the Federal Republic of Germany, mere participation in elections—even if the results do not reach the 5 percent minimum for representation—is sufficient for the party to receive a federal subsidy. Between 1980 and 1984, the Greens at the federal level received at least DM 40.5 million in public funds while raising only DM 15.3 million from membership fees and donations.[52] The reimbursement from public funds for their participation in the European parliamentary elections alone brought the Greens a total of DM 18.426 million, spread over several years, even though their campaign expenditures amounted to only DM 1 million.[53] To some extent this vast difference developed because the Greens' election campaign is considerably less expensive than that of the traditional parties. The large federal subsidy, however, has raised a number of legal problems, particularly as German law allows a political party to draw on only that portion of the funds matching the amount privately raised.

A law passed on February 15, 1984, subjects all political parties to public accounting of their finances. The accounts of the Greens show that in 1983 the party had a total income of DM 19,757,967.01, of which approximately half (DM 10,667,717.58) went to the federal party and the rest to the eleven state party organizations. Less than 10 percent (DM 1,885,995) came from membership fees, with the remainder divided among the following sources: DM 156,563.07 from contributions by caucus members; DM 316,994.09 from assets; DM 814,301.60 from public events, publications, and so on; DM 330,676.74 from loans; and DM 272,398.63 from miscellaneous sources for a total of DM 2,241,310.52. The lion's share of the income came from public funds—a total of DM 11,803,570.04, of which DM 8,057,495.33 went to the federal party. Additionally, the party was provided with an advance of DM 1,936,157.32 for its participation in the European parliamentary election campaign, for which it was to receive a total of DM 8.426 million.[54]

This largess from public funds undoubtedly led to a professionalization of the Green Party apparatus that the Greens themselves had not forseen, especially the hiring of full-time employees for the party and the caucus. On a per capita basis, the Greens are clearly the wealthiest party, with an income of DM 626 per member as opposed to DM 565 for the FDP, DM 368 for the CSU, DM 343 for the CDU, and DM 253 for the

SPD.[55] This situation results because the Greens have the fewest *members* but their federal subsidy is calculated on the basis of the number of *votes* received. It is nevertheless interesting to note that in the period from 1980 to 1983, the percentage of membership fees as part of the total party income was 12.1 for the Greens, 16 for the FDP, 19.1 for the CSU, 31.9 for the CDU, and 39.1 for the SPD.[56]

The slow increase in membership must be disappointing for the Greens; it did not rise in direct proportion to the party's election successes. At the time of its founding in January 1980 the Green Party was reported to have 10,000 members; this figure was used to determine the number of convention delegates. At the time of the Hagen Convention in 1982, the treasurer reported approximately 18,000 members, although the party secretariat later denied that any accurate figures existed during the 1980–81 period. In August 1982, there were said to be 22,000 members; a year later 25,000. The small increase in total membership between 1982 and 1983 was reportedly traceable to a cleanup of the membership list; despite a sizeable number of new members, others had dropped out. In July 1984, the membership was approximately 33,000.

The efforts of the Greens to increase membership have been rather modest. The stability of a party and the solidity of its foundation in the population can be gauged by comparing the number of members with the number of voters. In such a comparison, the Greens show themselves to be a cadre party, with a ratio of voters to members of 87:1, assuming 25,000 members at the time of the March 1983 elections. Table 10 shows this ratio in comparison with similar ratios in other German parties: 20:1 in the CSU and 16:1 in the SPD. By a similar basis of calculation, the ratio of Green voters to members was 44:1 in the 1980 elections; that is, 2.3 percent of the voters were members as compared to 1.2 percent in 1984. These figures are important in the type of parliamentary democracy existing in Germany because party conclaves in which only registered

TABLE 10
Levels of Party Organization

	Voters	Party Members	Ratio	Percent
Federal Republic				
Greens	2,167,431	25,000	87:1	1.2
SPD	14,865,807	950,000	16:1	6.4
CDU	14,857,680	734,082	20:1	4.9
CSU	4,140,865	182,665	23:1	4.4
FDP	2,706,942	78,763	34:1	2.9
Greens in various German states				
Schleswig-Holstein	91,098	1,200	76:1	1.3
Hamburg	90,174	780	116:1	0.9
Lower Saxony	278,597	3,600	77:1	1.3
Bremen	44,576	273	163:1	0.6
Northrhine-Westphalia	581,350	5,700	102:1	1.0
Hessen	218,898	2,800	78:1	1.3
Rhineland-Palatinate	113,185	1,300	87:1	1.1
Baden-Württemberg	389,863	4,500	87:1	1.2
Bavaria	323,901	5,400	60:1	1.7
Saarland	35,789	500	72:1	1.4
Berlin	90,653	2,800	32:1	3.1

Source: Helmut Fogt, "Grass-root Democracy, or Rule of the Activists?" in *Politische Vierteljahresschrift* (PVS), no. 1 (1984), p. 105. Membership figures for the Green Party according to information given to Fogt, April 9–Sept. 1983; see also *Süddeutsche Zeitung* of November 24, 1983; *Frankfurter Allgemeine Zeitung* of July 22, 1983. In the "voters" column, votes in the Bundestag election of 1983 are listed; Berlin votes are for the Alternative List on May 10, 1981.

Note: Figures for Green Party do not include those from Alternative Lists in Hamburg or Bremen. See List of Organizations for full names of parties.

party members can participate select the candidates for office. Although the Greens speak of participatory democracy that would give the maximum number of voters a chance to participate in its decision-making assemblies, in reality decisions are made by a small cadre of voters.

The Work of the Caucus

The financial resources annually available to the Green caucus in the Bundestag are quite substantial. According to the Bundestag budget, the Green caucus was allotted a budget of DM 7,229,090 for 1984, of which DM 556,090 is the basic amount for the caucus whereas the remainder is calculated on a per member basis. Added to this figure are training and education funds of DM 132,000 and additional funds made available for international cooperation.

According to its own financial statement of March 1984, the caucus has 54 members—double the number of seats—because the designated successors at the end of two years are counted. There is a staff of 75. For 1983, the caucus received approximately DM 5 million from public funds and an additional DM 330,000 for international activities.[57] The cost of the successor system was approximately DM 1.6 million; the remaining personnel costs about DM 1 million.[58]

In October 1983, the caucus decided to transfer annually DM 1 million from its funds to the party's 40 regional (or citizen and constituency) offices. Since the party could not legally make caucus funds available for this purpose, these DM 83,500 for each regional office were drawn from funds made available to each individual representative for the employment of staff, such as secretaries. Moreover, two-thirds of the funds made available to the individual members for office equipment and supplies were diverted to the so-called ecological funds. The Executive Committee of the party decided in February 1984 that these monies (DM 27,000 per month) would be used to pay for equipment and supplies at the regional offices. The caucus made available DM 500,000 for this purpose in 1983 and an additional DM 300,000 in February 1984.[59]

After the Greens entered the Bundestag, they adopted a plan creating working groups to advise on the most important political issues. These working groups were to be financed by the caucus. The assumption that these working groups are less advisory councils to the caucus than to the party would be difficult to disprove. The Greens are, therefore, running the danger of being accused of using dedicated caucus funds for party purposes. The automatic flow of public funds to political parties customary in the Federal Republic of Germany may well have been an important reason for the Greens to organize as a party and thereby find a way to finance the cost of a full-time party apparatus.

A look at the employment data (as of May 20, 1983) of the Green Bundestag members shows that nearly half of the 28 members were public servants: Ten were professionals in the civil service (5 teachers, 3 scientists, 1 professional soldier—who has now left the caucus—and one senior civil service employee); 2 were civil service clerical employees, and 1 was employed by the European Community; 4 were employees of political or social organizations, and 1 was a theologian. Private industry furnished 1 employee, and the private professions were represented by 4 Bundestag members, including 1 attorney. None was a housewife or self-employed artisan. Of the 28 members, 22 (78.6 percent) had a secondary-school leaving certificate; only the FDP with 82.9 percent exceeded this level of education (CDU/CSU 73.7 percent, SPD 56.4 percent).[60]

Equally interesting is a broader analysis of the employment picture to include the 28 successors and the 48 Green state legislators. Of these, 14 percent belonged to the administative and technological strata (engineers, architects, managers, judges, lawyers), and 5.8 percent were in the social services (health professionals, doctors, ministers of religion). The percentage of those not gainfully employed (students, housewives, pensioners, unemployed) is relatively high at 18.3.

Fifty-one and nine-tenths percent were active in education, the social sciences, and communications (teachers, lecturers, social scientists, and journalists). If the four intern lecturers are included in this category, 39 of the 104 (37.5 percent) were active in the teaching profession. Of the secondary-school teachers, 19 listed the subjects they teach: German led with 9, social science 8, history 6, sports 4, and religion 3. A total of 46.2 percent of all these Green legislators were employed in various aspects of the public service.

The Greens have taken a considerable number of parliamentary initiatives: Of about 60 bills introduced from the floor (i.e., without a draft from the executive branch), 22 originated with the Greens (SPD, 24). In submitting major questions to the government (29; SPD, 11) and in routine questions (241; SPD, 42), the Greens have far surpassed the major opposition party. In the handling of written and oral questions, most of which deal with the concerns of individual constituency districts (and are, therefore, of less concern to the Greens since all of them were elected by proportional representation on a national slate, rather than by winning in a specific district), the Greens fall far behind statistically. Nevertheless, they have submitted 730 such questions of a total of 7,611—a higher percentage than that of their members in the Bundestag. Additional details are listed in Table 11. The one multiparty bill shown on this table was the law amending the income and corporation tax and prohibiting the deduction of fines as legitimate corporate expenditures—a measure popular throughout the country.

An analysis of the subjects of Green parliamentary activity (Table 12) shows that its work was concentrated on three areas: security and defense, ecology (and the related subject of transportation), and health. Fifty-six of the 292 initiatives related to security, 58 to ecology (plus 4 on agricultural policy), 29 to atomic power and energy, 47 to transportation policy related to

TABLE 11
Draft Legislation, Major and Minor Inquiries, and Questions in the German Bundestag

	Total	CDU/CSU	CDU/CSU and FDP	FDP	SPD	Greens	CDU/CSU and FDP and SPD	All Parties	No Party Adherence Required
Draft bills from floor[a]	60	1	11		24	22	1	1	
Major inquiries	50		10		11	31			
Minor inquiries	296		13		42	241			
Questions	7,611	2,270		416	4,171	730			24

Source: Subject and Speech Index of the German Bundestag, July 15, 1984.

[a]Number of initiatives "from the middle of the house."

Note: See List of Organizations for full names of parties.

TABLE 12
Parliamentary Activity by the Greens (as of July 15, 1984)

	Draft Bills	Major Inquiries	Minor Inquiries	Total
Foreign policy and foreign relations	—	—	6	6
All-German relations	—	—	3	3
Security and defense policy/NATO/armed forces/weapons sales/ peace research/martial law	3	12	41	56
Conscientious objection/ alternative service	—	1	2	3
Third World/development aid	—	2	15	17
Ecology/environment/ sewage/chemical toxification/pollutants/ protection of landscape/ animals	8	3	47	58
Agriculture/ecofarming	—	2	2	4
Health/medicine/gene technology/food supply/ drug addiction	1	2	25	28
Atomic energy/reactor security/recycling nuclear waste/production of uranium	—	—	19	19
Energy/anthracite	—	4	6	10
Traffic policies	1	2	44	47
Law/administration of justice	3	1	6	9
Internal security/police/ right-wing extremism	1	—	6	9
Finance/economy/social policies	2	—	8	11
Handicapped/ rehabilitation	—	—	2	2
Women	1	—	1	2
Foreigners	1	—	—	1
Education	—	—	1	1
Miscellaneous	1	—	7	8
	22	31	241	294

ecological issues, and 29 to health policy. In other areas that the Greens claim are of special interest to them, they have been less active: handicapped policy, 2 initiatives; women's issues, 2; foreign workers, 1. In the field of education they submitted only one routine question. Issues of finance and the economy and social issues rated only 11 initiatives. These subjects appear to be of little interest, as is the case with general foreign policy issues and questions touching on the Third World. However, the thematic emphasis in the Bundestag is often determined by major events that make it necessary for smaller parties to react to the initiatives of the government or those of the other parties.

Aside from the one multiparty bill mentioned earlier, the Greens shied away from joint parliamentary initiatives with other parties except for routine parliamentary business, including the assignment of members to committees. Considerable debate took place within the Green Party about a joint resolution of all parties on April 11, 1984, condemning the continued occupation of Afghanistan by Soviet troops. Some within the Green Party, notably Bahro, were criticized for committing the Green caucus to this resolution, thereby joining a parliamentary majority that favored the NATO rearmament decision. They were accused of favoring U.S. and opposing Soviet interests.

The debate on the Afghanistan resolution illustrates the difficulties encountered by the Greens in achieving a consensus with the Bundestag majority. In the Green caucus, the resolution was supported by a narrow majority, and several members abstained when the resolution came to a vote on the floor. In only three other instances did the Greens join the other parties— one of them procedural and one minor.

An interesting situation arose in the third instance when the Greens demanded a sulphur-scrubbing facility for the power station at Buschhausen (Lower Saxony). Similar resolutions by the government and the SPD were withdrawn in favor of the resolution submitted by the Greens, which was adopted on June 27, 1984. On July 31, 1984, an extraordinary special session of the Bundestag followed in which the previous united position was reversed by the CDU/CSU-FDP majority after it became clear that the CDU government in Lower Saxony protested the decision, both feeling its authority impinged upon and pointing out that any implementation of the new law would lead to major difficulties.

A new style of dealing with the caucus leadership is apparently being adopted by some Green caucus members. Petra Kelly, Otto Schily, and Joschka Fischer were accused of seeking personal publicity in the media. At a caucus meeting on April 3, 1984, the leadership was entrusted to six women who had announced their joint candidacy. Waltraud Schoppe and Antje Vollmer were elected caucus speakers, Annemarie Borgmann as successor. The executive direction of the caucus (the role of whip) was entrusted to Christa Nickels, the position of assistant whip to Dr. Erika Hickel, and Heidemarie Dann was chosen as successor.

4
COMPOSITION OF
THE GREEN CAUCUSES

Divisions Within the Green Party

During its founding period, the Greens' policy of opposition to the existing social structure, especially to certain ecological problems, and to the North Atlantic Treaty Organization (NATO) decision on cruise and Pershing missiles served the party as central cohesive elements. By 1982, when the state governments in Hessen and Hamburg were unable to govern with a clear majority without the cooperation of the Greens, certain splits in party unity had come to the surface. As with all movements forced to base their policies on something other than pure negativism, the different ideological views of the party's component parts became visible. Until then they had frequently been concealed as had the fact that the Greens were a mixture of critics of capitalism and "conservative" critics of society and that these differing attitudes were at times patched together with great difficulty using theories of a "third way" between capitalism and communism. Clear differentiations between the various groups are difficult to make because their outlines are fluid. Nevertheless, four distinct groups emerge as of 1984: the "red-Greens," the "Green-red realists," the reform ecologists, and the fundamental oppositionists.

The Red-Greens

The red-Greens are also known as the ecosocialists or traditional socialists. The group encompasses members of former K-Groups but also the influential Z-Group, led by the spokesman of the party's federal executive, Trampert. Its supporters are primarily in the Berlin Alternative List but also in the Green-Alternative List in Hamburg. In these groups, the views of the alternative-rainbow groups are dominant. Ecology is only one subject among many which concern them. They also include women's issues, peace themes, and the support of an alternative culture. The view is dominant that the decisive and overarching question is the political-economic system (socialism vs. capitalism). Even though this group clearly favors socialist ideology, it seeks to distinguish itself from the communism of the DKP and from the German Democratic Republic by propagating a cultural revolution: It favors life in an alternative society. It holds that only changes in property ownership, and thereby in the exercise of power, can effectively counter an ecological catastrophe.

The supporters of this group emphasize participatory democracy as an element of Green policy and defend the ideas of local democratic councils (as these were preached before World War I under the heading of "Rätedemokratie") as the source of imperative mandates. They see parliament primarily as an instrument of class struggle: a platform for new social, extra-parliamentary movements. There is no well-established line of demarcation between this group and the militants.

Green-Red Realists

The group of Green-red realists is occasionally known as the green reform socialists or the radical reformers. It counts among its members such party leaders as Joschka Fischer and Otto Schily. Although they favor socialist ideas, they emphasize ecological issues. They do not fear future shared political responsibility and have, therefore, identified themselves with the decision of the Hessen Green Party to support the election of Socialist Minister President Börner by their vote in the Hessen legislature. They desire to use opportunities offered by membership in parliament to take small steps, that is, to accept such progress as might be pragmatically possible rather than to remain in total opposition. The members of this group are also dedicated to participatory democracy, although they generally reject the idea of rotation at the end of two years of parliamentary service. They believe that limited cooperation with the SPD is possible.

The Reform Ecologists

The reform ecologist group is primarily represented in the Green parties of Baden-Württemberg, Lower Saxony, and to some extent in Northrhine-Westphalia. It seeks a "third way" between capitalism and communism. It attaches greater importance to ecological issues than to those of the politicoeconomic system. It has a positive attitude toward parliament as an institution, is prepared in principle to accept political responsibility, and regards the Green representatives in the Bundestag as more than the extended arm of a social movement. As a rule, it favors nonviolence.

This group primarily includes the ecolibertarians who on February 26, 1984, formed a "political current both within and outside the Green party."[61] The founding document of this group was signed by a number of prominent Germans: Wolf-Dieter Hasenclever and Winfried Kretschmann (both of whom had previously served in the legislature of Baden-Württemberg), Ernst Hoplitschek (a former member of the Green's federal executive), and Thomas Schmid (an editor of the quarterly *Freibeuter*). The ecolibertarians believe that control over the means of production is of secondary importance whereas industrialism and its consequences are the primary problems. Social issues are considered to be secondary because they are "issues resulting from industrialism." As a result, the group demands an ecological policy, historically new and unique: "Reduced production, less state involvement, fewer promises, fewer applications of technical know-how, etc."

The ecolibertarians support individual responsibility and promote their intention to strengthen the forces that favor self-help. They seek to reverse the government's role in welfare and social well-being, claiming that the welfare state is two-faced: while helping, it creates dependency; while assisting the needy, it robs them of their independence. They reject the "social democratic fetish of social security" as a point of departure. The ecolibertarians uniformly favor parliamentary democracy and the politics of dialogue. They have no hesitation in negotiating with any other political forces; although they are willing to negotiate with the SPD, they warn of the danger of becoming that party's junior partner. Individual representatives have even included the idea of cooperating with the Christian parties, at least in principle. They seek to bring about a reform of basic policies, including "decentralization, devolution of state ownership, self-help and a rejection of industrialism." The ecolibertarians claim that within the Green Party, the cultural concepts of the alternative movement have become dominant in nearly all areas of activity and that the disenchanted masses of several Communist groups had infiltrated the party, using skills learned as cadres in their former affiliations.

Fundamental Oppositionists

In addition to Petra Kelly and Bundestag member Milan Horacek, the group of fundamental oppositionists also houses the former GDR citizen Rudolf Bahro. Although these people do not oppose parliamentary democracy per se, they do in principle reject joint parliamentary responsiblity, as, for instance, joining the coalition in Hessen. They like to call themselves radical ecologists and oppose ties to any single other party. For them, the primary issue is human survival. In face of the immediate threat to the human race posed by unlimited exploitation, desecration, progressive chemical poisoning of the environment, and so on, they give this issue greater priority than the class struggle. Bahro, who particularly stresses the continuity of mankind and condemns the consequences of industrialization, has great reservations about the German Trade Union Federation, which he has called "one of the battleships of destructive industrialization."[62] The real task of an ecological party, according to Bahro, consists of "separating our system from the world market. We must move into a non-participating role relative to the industrial system until it is destroyed by the weight of 5 million unemployed."[63]

Bahro, who is a major proponent of this group, often unmistakingly expresses the view that he rejects a policy of small steps toward reform. In connection with the unemployment issue, for instance, he stated: "It is not our job to save or create jobs in the industrial system, to furnish people with wages and bread—rather it is to reduce the amount of work being performed for the existing anonymous market with its profit motive and to bring about its total restructuring."[64] "There is not too little work but rather much too much."[65]

The fundamental oppositionists want to use parliament for the propagation of a new ideology, for the "principle of living," for a "new life style not only in the Western world but also in people's personal life."[66] For this reason they proclaim "better, non-exploiting styles of life, alternative life styles, non-violent relationships with others and with one self, a policy of neighborly love, of love,"[67] and "a departure from the patriarchial society." At the same time they reject atomic energy, nuclear deterrence, and a wasteful economy. These ideas have all the characteristics of a theory of salvation, with strong views opposed to all civilizing and industrializing tendencies. Petra Kelly has even spoken of a "spiritual element in an ecologically unifying policy."[68] These views result in a demand for a policy of nonviolence and for an erotic society.[69]

Ecology as the Guiding Science

Ecological, social, participatorily democratic, and nonviolent are the four fundamental principles on which the Green Party has based its federal program. The color green signifies the ecological demands of the party. Ecological issues were initially vigorously pursued by the citizen initiatives of the 1970's and adopted by the Green Party then being formed as its lead idea. In all parts of the population there was increasing recognition of the dangers of environmental destruction. What started initially as fear of radioactivity from nuclear power plants and nuclear energy turned in the years that followed into an increasing number of reports of catastrophies (transformation of landscapes into cement highways, toxification of the soil, chemical pollution of the environment, problems of waste disposal, endangering of plants and animals, presence of dangerous pollutants in factories and offices, and so on). A dramatic climax took place in the early 1980's with the increased recognition that Europe's forests were dying from acid rain and other pollution sources.

Even though the traditional parties were concerned increasingly with environmental issues and even had some success (such as improvement of the water quality of rivers and lakes), the Greens took this issue, which already concerned the population, and gave it priority attention. Even recent polls show that people ascribe a high level of competence to the Greens on this issue. An EMNID Institute poll of August 1984 gave the Greens 40 percent of popular approval on this issue as opposed to 15 percent for the CDU/CSU and only 11 percent for the SPD.[70]

In the absence of these urgent ecological issues, the Greens would surely not have been able to garner more than 5 percent of the votes in the March 1984 Bundestag elections. The wave of ecological concern was launched throughout the world and especially in the Federal Republic by the scientifically debatable book *The Limits of Growth* by U.S. author Donnella Meadows et al. and published in 1972 by the Club of Rome.[71] The book by Herbert Gruhl, then a member of the CDU/CSU caucus in the Bundestag, entitled *The Plundering of the Planet—The Balance Sheet of Anguish in Our Policies* was one of the bestsellers among political literature in the Federal Republic of Germany.[72] Similar interest was engendered by the book *The End or the Turning Point* by Erhard Eppler, a member of the left wing of the SPD.[73] The sensitivity of the people of the Federal Republic to ecological issues is also shown by the fact that the *Global 2000* report by a group of U.S. experts to the president of the United States received wider distribution in the Federal Republic than in the United States; within 15 months of publication, 420,000 copies were distributed in Germany.[74]

It would not be accurate to view the Green Party solely as an ecological party, devoted only to ecological issues. But the color of the party is its dominant element and the sole common denominator between its divergent wings. It should also be added that many former members of Communist groups joined the Green Party in the late 1970's after the popular resonance to its ecological demands became clear. While the party was being formed, a number of community groups and state organizations used adjectives like rainbow or multicolored to refer to themselves because they had found their base not only in the green of ecology but also in the red of those who wanted to alter the politicoeconomic system in the name of socialism, the lilac of the feminist movement, and the black of the anarchist Spontis. Only the convergence of the political colors created a strong German Green Party and established a presence in parliament for the various protest movements, in which different colors are predominant depending on the momentary political situation.

The Green Party has achieved maximum consensus on the ecological issue. The idea of nature is at the core of ecological ideology and at the center of Green philosophy.[75] According to the Greens' federal platform, which is based on "the laws of nature and especially on the recognition that in a limited world growth cannot be unlimited,"[76] ecological policy is defined "as an understanding of ourselves and our environment as a part of nature." Human life, too, is tied to the "regulatory cycles of the eco-system," making it mandatory that its stability not be destroyed. The Greens want to end "exploitation and the continued robbing of the goods of nature and its resources" as well as the "destructive invasion of nature's natural circulatory system." They advocate opposition to the "exploitation of nature and of humans by humans." The Greens therefore demand "a policy of active partnership with nature and with the human race."[77]

To Carl Amery, who provided the Green-Alternative movement with a philosophical basis, ecology is a primary science that "firmly and demonstrably anchors human beings and human society into the existing network of planetary relationships."[78] In her 1982 book *The Philosophy of the Greens*, Manon Maren-Grisebach, formerly one of the three speakers for the Greens, termed ecology a "scientific base, a basis for action and a field which can be subjected to examination and proof, meeting the exacting demands of Western scientific processes." She continued: "But ecology is demanding. At the risk of our own destruction, we cannot ignore its insights; we are not free to act at will because we are forced to obey laws which reach beyond our selfs and deal with our very existence. This is not a belief, a conviction or a draft for social action but knowledge itself."[79]

As much as the Greens mistrust the products of science, it is astonishing to note the deep trust they have in the natural science of ecology. Manon Maren-Grisebach tends to lend ecology almost religious characteristics because it provides "such a firm foundation" as well as "knowledge" and "the interaction of all earthly processes."[80] For many Greens, the preoccupation with ecology has become a doctrine of salvation, making possible a comprehensive interpretation of the world. Some demand "a search for an order which will link human society and economy harmoniously with the factors of nature";[81] for "a social harmonization of human beings through the incorporation of their existence into nature by a benevolent understanding of its forces";[82] for "an ecological humanism which provides at once an anchor of safety and a steering rudder, taking the space ship earth from the dangers of sea and air, preventing a disaster, and returning it to its proper course guided by winds and waves."[83]

Although the student revolt of the 1968 generation was motivated by a bourgeois belief in progress, the ecological movement lives to a large extent on findings of catastrophe and a philosophy of eschatology, on a fear of the end of the world. These apocalyptic ideas not only spread fear; they produce images of enemies and a search for those guilty for bringing about the catastrophe. Depending on the local situation, these enemies are either the entire industrial system (as seen by the Fundamentalists) or the so-called late capitalism (as seen by the red-Greens). In part, this ecological ideology also stands in opposition to modern rationalism and the scientific technological civilization that it has created.[84]

The ecological ideology—when it is presented as the sole truth, applicable to all—leads in the long run to a conflict with the modern, liberal, constitutional state in which differing philosophies are acceptable. Although no generalized identity can be established, the ecological ideology has a number of similarities with Marxism. Both proceed from a generally accepted "truth" (scientific socialism in one case, ecological ideology in the other), and both clearly identify an enemy (capitalism in one, and the industrial system or the atomic state in the other). Both proceed from an assumption of catastrophe (degradation of the working class in one and collapse of the ecosystem earth in the other), and both claim the promise of salvation (the withering away of the state in one, unity with nature in the other).[85] Both also require a change in the methods of production for the achievement of their respective goals. (See Socialistic Council–Democratic Ideology section of Chapter 5.)

The success of a political movement increases as it is able

to convey the impression that it provides conclusive answers to political dangers and catastrophies. Such slogans as "Euroshima" and "Battlefield Europe," which were used in connection with the fight against the NATO rearmament decision, clearly show how the fear of catastrophe was used for political ends.

There can be no doubt that the ideology of ecology posseses quasi-religious characteristics for many Greens. The book by the Austro-American physicist-philosopher Fritjof Capra, *The Turning Point*—which was widely read by those in Germany favoring an alternative life-style—shows the way toward spirituality and mysticism. Capra differentiated between superficial environmental concerns and deep ecology. The former is concerned solely with more effective controls and better management of the natural environment and its use by humanity, whereas the deep ecology movement recognizes that the ecological balance requires deep-seated changes in the assumption of the role of human beings in the planetary ecosystem. Capra stated:

> When the concept of the human spirit is understood in this sense, as the mode of consciousness in which the individual feels connected to the cosmos as a whole, it becomes clear that ecological awareness is truly spiritual. Indeed, the idea of the individual being linked to the cosmos is expressed in the Latin root of the word religion, *religiare* (to bind strongly), as well as in the Sanscrit *yoga*, which means union.[86]

Capra's fame on the German alternative scene began with the publication of his slim volume *The Tao of Physics,* in which he pointed out the relationship between modern quantum physics and a number of Taoist insights.[87]

Ecology, then, is for many of the adherents of the Green movement a normative science that not only analyzes what is but also delivers prescriptions for what shall be. An ecological ideology seen in this light meets the need of many Greens for a holistic philosophy—"and it includes feelings from the deepest sources of human need."[88] As a science, it promises a utopian "peace with nature." This promised utopia is precisely the reason for the success of the Green movement, for it offers attempts at explanations that, together with expectations of salvation, seem to provide philosophical answers for the condition of the world. Young people in particular often search for such a utopia, for such final truths.

5

THE POLICIES
OF THE GREENS

What Do the Greens in Parliament Want?

Within the Green and alternative movements the realization has increasingly taken hold that influence can be exercised by operating within the system—by holding elected seats in parliaments. By following this approach party members would have opportunities to present themselves to public view in parliamentary debates, television interviews and discussions, election spots, and so on. Although a portion of the Green movement favors parliamentary democracy, others regard participation in elections solely as a tactical variant for the achievement of political power.

Parliamentary Versus Representative Democracy

No doubt within the Green Party strong antiparliamentary tendencies will continue, especially among those members who come from the rainbow or alternative scene. For example, the former chairman of the Hamburg Green-Alternative List (GAL), Thomas Ebermann, favored the concept that "societal changes must for the most part not be routed through parliamentary channels." In response to the question whether the GAL would be willing to consider a compromise, he stated that he did not consider this "an appropriate objective."[89] But a parliamentary democracy is only viable when it can accept the idea of compromise in principle. The rejection of parliamentary democracy was also stated frankly by the former chairman of the Berlin Alternative List, Klaus-Jürgen Schmidt: "The institution of parliament does not permit the exercise of direct democracy which we seek. We have no plan at this time for a substitute but we must consider it. The way in which that institution is now organized, so far removed from the interests of the people and working through committees—all this has little to do with direct democracy."[90]

The differing views of parliamentary democracy within the Green Party may be contrasted by comparing the views of Gertrud Schilling, who later became a member of the Hessen legislature ("It is the goal of the Greens to do away with parliament and to practice direct democracy"),[91] and those of Petra Kelly ("We do not exist to do away with parliament. We do want to make parliamentary democracy more trustworthy and more transparent. The Greens want to alter the existing parliaments").[92] The participation of the Greens in parliamentary elections was described as follows in a publication by the Gray Cell of Berlin, an alternative group of West Berlin students who were born between 1959 and 1961:

> The remainder of a group of radicals, oriented toward participatory democracy, which has stayed within the Green Party, is intending to enter parliament in order to create chaos within it. It intends to make clever use of bourgeois mass communications systems to propagandize against parliament, to present their fundamentally opposing point of view, to misuse the trust, power and competence of parliament, to lay it open to ridicule, to develop its own authority structures and to bring fantasy to power.[93]

The official program of the Greens does not oppose parliamentary democracy outright but ranks it in second place after participatory activities. The preamble to the party's federal program contains the following: "We consider it necessary to supplement extraparliamentary activities by participating in communal and state legislatures and in the federal parliament." The Greens, it follows, desire to give their political alternatives "publicity and meaning" within the parliamentary bodies. The allegiance to parliamentary democracy in the program of the Greens is rather weak, however, and the party tends to criticize the failure of parliaments to function, requiring that "opposition" be brought into them by "appropriate action."[94] "Extra-parliamentary opposition needs to be strengthened and motivated."

The Greens view representative democracy in contradistinction to participatory democracy. The latter is to be realized through a "new type of party organization."[95] Central to this thought is the "permanent control of all office holders, representatives and institutions by the membership-at-large and their replacement at any time in order to make the organization and its policies transparent to all and to counter the ability of individuals to act on their own volition."[96] The decisions of the membership-at-large must be given "absolute priority." These statements in the federal program and similar ones in the programs of the various *Länder* uniformly lead to an imposed mandate and to the concept of rotation under which the party limits the length of time any representative can serve.

Along with this concept, the party believes in a policy of consensus. Under it, minority views cannot be excluded from the formation of policy and subjects should ideally be discussed until unanimity is achieved. Furthermore, the party endorses open membership throughout the party. The question, therefore, arises whether the participatory democracy policy of the Greens, the principle of rotation and the limitations it places on the powers of its representatives in the various legislative bodies, does not lead to the type of oligarchial control by political party organizations that Robert Michels feared as early as 1911.[97]

Several critical points need to be examined in this connection: According to Article 33 of the Basic Law of the Federal Republic of Germany, "members of parliament are representative of the entire nation. They are not bound by directives and guidances but are subject solely to their own conscience." Neither the imposed mandate nor the principle of rotation, each of which demand absolute obedience to the party, is compatible with these provisions. The federal caucus of the Greens at Sindelfingen decided, in opposition to these constitutional requirements, that "the Greens in the Bundestag are bound by the decisions of the party's federal assembly and its executive committee. Violations of these decisions are grounds for expulsion from the federal caucus."[98] Of course, in practice the traditional parties also exercise considerable coercion on individual representatives. The desire for renomination alone is a major cause for acceding to party wishes, but examples recur of representatives who do not follow the party leadership. The total control of individual representatives by an imposed mandate, on the other hand, represents an institutionalized lack of confidence in them, a constant fear that they may be corrupted by the "powers." The Greens appear unable to comprehend that a democracy can be created by trust in the personal integrity of the elected representatives and in the work they perform.

Rotation

Participatory democracy stands in contrast to representative democracy. In the latter, representatives are elected for a specific term and at the end of that term must seek a renewal of their mandate from their constituency. Although there is no continuing control by the voters in election districts, indirect controls are exercised through the expression of public opinion and the action of representatives of other parties. This system, too, has its faults, such as the occasional nomination of unsuitable candidates. The focus, therefore, remains on the quality of the representation.

Wolf-Dieter Hasenclever, former leader of the Greens in the Baden-Württemberg legislature and a pronounced opponent of rotation, abandoned his plans to stand for reelection in 1984 because he was unwilling to accept rotation and the imposed mandate. "As far as I am concerned," he stated, "the lack of trust disguised by arguments about participatory democracy is nothing more than a dog-in-the-manger attitude."[99] This distrust by the party in its parliamentary representatives, exemplified by the imposed mandate, has an additional aspect: Those representatives who are able to obtain favorable or effective media coverage are often accused of being status hungry. This accusation was primarily directed at Petra Kelly, the best known Green politician. The fear that an individual representative could gain too much status resulted in expressions of distrust and jealousy and in a cold shoulder in personal relationships. Petra Kelly, who had been one of the spokespersons for the caucus for a year, was summarily dismissed from this role—she was the first to suffer the consequences of the fear that the party could produce mandarins.

The imposed mandate does nothing to strengthen the individuality of the parliamentary representatives or to support their keenness or creativity. It tends rather to develop the opportunistic party functionaries who shift to the view of the prevailing majority and do not come to public attention because they might have a different point of view—in short, party functionaries "smooth as an eel."

The principle of rotation—which was also applied to the party executive a year after the party's entry into parliament—overlooks the fact that in a complicated democracy demanding specialization, politicians need time to learn and to gain experience and an understanding of detail. These are essential preconditions for responsible action. They represent the minimum of continuity essential in members of a legislative body to enable it to exercise effective control over arbitrary action by the executive. The consequences of rotation, however, are the inflexible establishment of a political position since the constant need to begin anew prevents efficiency, even if one were to ignore that the predetermined short period in office acts psychologically as a deterrent to achievement rather than as its motivation. Views of a political ideal embodied in this principle presuppose so total an identity between the voters and their elected representatives as to be incompatible with conditions in a modern world of specialization.

Those favoring rotation point to the reported success of so-called "communal office organizations" where all people work with designated successors who take their places at specific times. But the argument is illusory. In the Green Party, many of the successors have different areas of prime interest; moreover, many of those now in office have already stated that they intend to become ordinary party members at the conclusion of their terms of office and do not wish to switch jobs with their successors. German legislation concerning reemployment rights after a period of service in the legislature guarantees such reemployment for only one year after service and could, therefore, result in an undue dependency on the party itself if it is the last previous employer. In communal office organizations, this situation often leads to unbearable working conditions; the constant exercise of controls places those who are to be succeeded under great psychological strain.

Greens Versus Parliament

Who constitutes this party base that is to make all the important decisions? Is it the 2 million voters who have sent the Green Party into the Bundestag, the various state legislatures, and the European parliament? Or is it the party activists? Even in the case of the Greens, in spite of their relatively active membership participation, the same tendency that exists in the traditional parties is noticeable: signs of fatigue are evident. At many membership meetings only 10 to 20 percent of the base is present and often different people attend different events, so that majorities on any particular issue can easily be the result of coincidence. But are the functionaries, who are the minority in this and other parties, representative of the party solely because they attend every meeting? Prof. Ralf Dahrendorf accurately pointed out that in every organized participatory democracy the nonelected functionaries play a special role, resulting in the danger that this type of democracy "can be transformed into an oligarchy of activists whom no one has authorized to act."[100]

The ideas of participatory democracy held by the Greens are illusory in a modern society and necessarily lead to a replacement of the people by an elite minority cadre. Such a system could function only through the total and constant participation of all members in all areas of activity, thereby preventing independent action by activist minorities. But the demands of such a system on the individual are too great. They require that in addition to family obligations and job and leisure time activities every member also accept permanent political responsibility. Added to this must be the recognition that decisions taken at plenary meetings can be manipulated because a small, well-organized, active, and eloquent minority is often able to make an emotional appeal to the majority and thereby obtain its consent to the minority's own narrow goals.[101]

Especially problematical is the principle of consensus. It can be used without difficulty only when all are in fact united in their point of view. When opposition arises, discussion stretches through many hours and even days until the debaters reach the point of exhaustion. At this point, the instrument created for the protection of the minority becomes an instrument of extortion directed against the majority. In many cases it leads to compromises not reflective of the majority view.[102]

In actual practice, what is the Greens' relationship to the majority decisions in parliament? In an interview in the weekly *Der Spiegel*, Otto Schily referred to an expression by the theologian Dorothee Sölle according to which "the minority is paralyzed by a purely quantitative understanding of democracy." Schily questioned the rule of the majority by stating that "democracy is so static as to be forced to respect any statistical majority. The minority must do everything in its power to bring about change. Particularly when there is fear of the very continuation of human existence, the qualitatively superior minority may carry more weight than the quantitative majority."[103]

This argumentation, setting the position of the minority (the qualitative minority) in opposition to the quantitative majority, reflects a view of politics that claims absolute priority for one point of view, thereby questioning in the long-run the pluralism of a modern democratic society. It holds one point of view to be qualitatively superior, a position used by Joschka Fischer when he justified the right of resistance: "I shall continue to accept the consequences of breaking the law in order to create humane relationships."[104]

The contempt for democratic ways displayed by a portion of the Green caucus became apparent during the debate on the NATO rearmament issue when an attempt was made to coordinate extraparliamentary protests with the debate in the Bundestag. The minutes of the special session of the Green caucus on November 20, 1983, clearly showed that the Greens entered the rearmament debate with a scenario that also included a "confrontation with the security forces."[105] It was intended to circumvent the police cordon around the Bundestag building (which had been ordered to permit uninterrupted debate) by demonstrations in that area outside the parliament building in which demonstrations had been prohibited. The incident would of necessity have led to a confrontation between the demonstrators and the police. The intensive preparation for the debate by the Green caucus was directed toward the provocation of tumultuous scenes, for which the caucus of the government parties was to be blamed. The minutes specified that

> Dieter Burgmann suggested that a scenario for the debate be developed and that toward the end of the debate provocative statements be made so that tumult and disturbances would originate with the other parties. Everyone should prepare state-

ments which could lead to such disturbances. Such statements would, for example, challenge the government's legitimate right to make such a decision, doubt the government's commitment to peace, and suggest that the government had failed to understand the issues.

According to the minutes, the caucus secretary at the time, Joschka Fischer, stated that the "debate should end in a definite climax but that heat needed to be generated from the beginning."

The lack of respect that a portion of the Greens have for parliament was also noticeable on May 18, 1983, when a debate period was set aside for questions from young people. Twenty-five hecklers, who had entered the parliament building at the invitation of the Greens, participated. Some of them threw paint bombs at the national symbol, the eagle, and attacked the ushers. A report made to a select committee of the Bundestag made clear that those causing the disturbances were "professionals." Those carrying placards and defacing the hall were protected against the marshals by others in the group.[106] They called the ushers "fascist pigs" and threatened them. All were between 21 and 35 years old and resided in Berlin (where, however, only one of them had been born). Fifteen had criminal records, including several disturbances of the peace, formation of criminal associations, and attempting to free convicts. According to news reports, the group had an ideological affinity to the notorious Red Army Faction.[107]

The reaction of the Green caucus to this event was divided. Representative Waltraud Schoppe declared in a press statement: "I admit that I was shocked because I, as a member of the Bundestag, had made the decision to conduct politics in a different way. But we must be clear: the young people who threw paint on the eagle threw the evidence of their disrespect. No matter how it may disturb us, we have to take it seriously. Our society lives in fear. Fear does not end merely by people claiming that it does not exist."

Are the Policies of the Greens Nonviolent?

One of the four pillars of Green policy is nonviolence. The federal platform states: "We seek a nonviolent society in which the suppression of humans by humans and the use of force by humans against humans has ended. Our highest principle states that humane goals cannot be achieved by inhumane methods." But violence has not been as disdained as might be assumed from a reading of these sentences, for they continue with the statement that

> the principle of nonviolence does not exclude the fundamental right of self-defense nor social resistance in any number of guises. It does not exclude active social resistance, nor imply passive behavior by its victims. The principle of nonviolence, on the contrary, holds that human beings may defend their vital interests against an authoritarian power structure. Under certain circumstances this might not only legitimate resistance to the demands of the state but make such resistance (e.g. sit-down strikes, road blocks, blocks of vehicular traffic) a necessity.

It is true that within the Green Party a strong group exists that is seriously opposed to any form of violence. Former state legislator Hasenclever, for instance, stated that people committed to force have no place in the Green Party.[108] But as early as fall 1981, a peace manifesto published by the Greens did not exclude the use of force against property as a method of political action. It stated: "We shall not be irritated by the representatives of the authorities which seek to portray legal, nonviolent action as violence in diguise."[109] Roland Vogt, at the time one of the spokespersons of the Greens, declared that the principle of direct nonviolent action excluded all violence against another person but that damage to property could happen now and then; he did term the indiscriminate smashing of windows as a misunderstanding of the principle of damage to property as a political expression.[110]

Petra Kelly, on the other hand, complained to the caucus in February 1985 about the contradictory behavior of some Greens with regard to the principle of nonviolence. She referred to the reprimand by the Greens of retired General Gert Bastian, a former member of the Green caucus, for a statement in which he had criticized the unprovoked excesses that had taken place on the occasion of the visit of Vice-President George Bush to Krefeld on June 15, 1983. Bastian had termed the action as a "violation of the principle of nonviolence." Kelly's complaint referred to a letter signed by 18 members of the Hamburg Green-Alternative List sent to *die tageszeitung* in which they had stated: "We are in absolute disagreement with Gert Bastian's action to dissociate himself from those who gave expression to their opposition to American war policy by throwing paint, stink bombs and some rocks at the concluding ceremony of the German-American peace festival in Krefeld. Even those who are unwilling to approve all forms of the resistance practiced at Krefeld should be guided by the common goal in their attitude toward the militant parts of the movement." Kelly also took issue with a press statement that had called those who had committed the violent acts part of the peace movement.[111]

The Alternative List Berlin, which is closely affiliated with the federal Green Party, was unwilling to reject the violent demonstrations that took place on the occasion of President Ronald Reagan's visit to Berlin on June 11, 1982; at a membership meeting on August 24, 1982, the group avoided taking a firm position in favor to totally nonviolent forms of resistance.[112] Not surprisingly this group did not reject the idea of militant resistance. In a declaration of its delegate council on August 10, 1983, it unanimously approved participation in the preparation on nonviolent action in connection with the NATO rearmament decision but tolerated violent acts by stating that "it did not deem it appropriate to impose its policies on others who, on the basis of their own political experiences, had developed different forms of resistance." It considered it important to discuss the total extent of all forms of resistance within the movement in a spirit of communality and solidarity.[113] Rainer Trampert, one of the three party chairmen, encouraged members to "violate the legalities established by the state."[114]

Resistance

A few additional remarks need to be made at this point. The Greens and the peace movement, when acting against the fulfillment of the NATO rearmament decision, again and again used the term "resistance" and wittingly or unwittingly served to create a tie to the resistance against Nazism during the Third Reich.[115] Those using that term in today's context fail to differentiate between the democracy now in existence in the Federal Republic of Germany and the dictatorship of 1933–1945 and intimate that they too are resistance fighters. This approach basically defames those who endangered their lives in resistance to the dictatorship and those in other countries who still do so. In totalitarian systems there is no constitutional right to form an opposition or to exercise it. Any direct or indirect comparison of a free political system with that of a dictatorship is basically dishonest.[116]

In a democracy, in a state of law, the citizens have many opportunities for protest, up to and including an appeal to the courts. Those approving the right of resistance, as propagated by the Greens, base their argument on Article 20, Paragraph 4, of the Basic Law. This article, which is related to a state of emergency, accords "all Germans the right of resistance" if the basis for the governmental system provided for in the Basic Law no longer exists and "no other remedial action is possible."

No one could possibly claim that the implementation of the NATO rearmament decision would remove domestic tranquility from the Federal Republic of Germany. On the contrary, the NATO alliance's task is to protect the country's basic liberal, democratic structure against all foreign dangers. The adherents of the Green Party and the peace movement, on the other hand, argued that rearmament has irreversible consequences because it creates a new irreversible level of military threat. This argument can be refuted. Only military parity can successfully bring about disarmament conferences and an end to the arms race. Why should such negotiations not lead to sensible results? Who can claim the political wisdom to proclaim the right of resistance to a parliamentary decision designed to develop this course of action? In a representative democracy, political decisions are delegated to the elected representatives who, for a specified period of time, assume the decision-making responsibility for all the citizens. Moreover, the German voters were aware at least six months prior to the decision on rearmament what policy the governing coalition would advocate. The claim of the Greens and the peace movement that a popular majority was against the decision was not reflected in any binding process representing the popular will. Opinion polls cannot be substituted for the parliamentary decision-making process.

Anyone demanding the right of resistance against this decision must of necessity extend this right to any other citizens who oppose parliamentary decisions with irreversible consequences. Included among these are the arguments against the acceptance as permanent of the present eastern frontiers, decisions frequently denounced by right-wing expellee organizations but not part of the Green agenda.

Calls for the right of resistance blur the elementary differences between a democracy and a dictatorship. The attributes of a democracy are freedom of opinion and freedom of the press, competition for popular support by organizations such as political parties, the right to form and exercise opposition, the independence of the judiciary, legislative and judicial controls over the administration, and the absence of similar controls over private associations such as trade unions. At the same time, democracy demands that all are equal under the law, a dictum that includes respect for the rights of others. In the establishment of these principles the state has a "monopoly of authority." Although this may not be the happiest of expressions, it embodies the principle that the state and its laws are in the end solely responsible for the orderly resolution of conflicts, for maintaining the rules of democracy, for equal treatment of all its citizens under the law, and for the protection of the individual's right to freedom and dignity. It might be better to speak of a "monopoly of law" and to draw on it to explain the duty of the state to guarantee legality and equity within democratic society. This monopoly of law and authority is based on specific legislation and on the constitution (see Article 28, Paragraph 3, of the Basic Law).

Civil Disobedience

As has already been emphasized, one of the basic legal principles of a democracy is the equal treatment under law of all its citizens. This tenet excludes the application of different treatment to violators of law in the cause of political action. Were this not the case, those with specific political arguments for their violations of the law would legally be accorded a higher moral standing than others. They would be placed in the privileged role of not being bound by generally applicable laws. A modern state, by accepting such a dual standard, would be condoning the idea of selective application of laws and thereby relinquish its basic function of assuring legal equality and protection.

The definition of civil disobedience favored by the Greens and the peace movement is based on the theory of "structural force." According to the Norwegian peace researcher Johan Galtung, force is exercised when human beings are influenced so that "their actual somatic and psychological realization is less than their potential."[117] Some adherents of civil disobedience point to Galtung and demand a counterforce against the structural force, thereby accepting in principle the use of force, even if only against property. They overlook the fact that force can be not only physical but also psychological. Even coercion, such as the illegal blocking of streetcars, must be seen as the use of force.

As a rule, those favoring civil disobedience within the Green movement base their actions on decisions of conscience, on the necessity to prevent decisions with irreversible consequences. The threshold in favor of a possible violation of law is lowered, however, when a protagonist and propagandist of civil disobedience frequently cited by the Greens, Theodor Ebert, expressed the view that even in something less than a decision of conscience, civil disobedience may have its use: "The idea of civil disobedience was originally developed in order to protest questions of political conscience effectively. But the process may be applied in less serious cases of conflict. Even if no highly valued reasons of conscience can be cited but when there is simply anger about unjust conditions, civil disobedience may be an acceptable expression of the social compact."[118]

Such a sentence is revealing, for it indicates that whatever is an acceptable part of the social compact is determined by those who accord to themselves a greater right than they do to others and thereby negate the accepted democratic order. In this view, every person decides for himself or herself what is an acceptable part of the social compact. This is an example of an elitist philosophy, occasionally found in certain intellectual circles, which elevates the demand for the acceptance of the views of the speaker and disdains the resolution of conflict through law.

Summary

The Basic Law provides minorities with manifold opportunities to present their views and with the unquestioned right to persuade the majority to accept their position. The constitutional law of a democratic state also guarantees the protection of minorities and does not permit the subordination of this guarantee to the will of the majority. Such protection includes the right to freedom of speech (Article 51, Paragraph 1), freedom of assembly (Article 8), and the freedom to demonstrate. Only when the political actions of a state no longer provide for the protection of the weak and of minorities or leads to their abuse—when democracy itself ceases to exist—only then is there justification for the resistance for which provision is made in the Basic Law.

The Greens and Economic Policy

The two basic pillars of Green policy are ecological and social. According to the party's federal platform, the two are closely interrelated. The most important Green document on problems of the economy and the ecology is the program adopted at the Stuttgart-Sindelfingen convention January 15–16, 1983, entitled "Against Unemployment and Social Disarmament—To Work Sensibly and Live in Solidarity." Declarations and questions in parliament and the state legislatures by the Greens about this program tend to emphasize its provisions on environmental protection. A close look at the Sindelfingen program, however, makes clear that a majority of the Greens are increasingly wedded to a party with left-wing socialist ideas. The program calls for an economy that is structured ecologically and socially and in which decisions are made through participatory democracy. It expresses the view that capitalistic as well as the so-called materialistically socialistic forms of society are failures since both systems are variations of an estranged "factory and office society" that are guided by a desire for a "destructive industrial growth."[119]

In the Sindelfingen program, the Greens demand a social economy and see as its function "to serve the material, social and cultural needs of the individual and society." They developed the idea of a third way between capitalism and what they called materialistic socialism, both of which they rejected. They proceeded from the assumption that the existing situation with regard to property and control of the means of production is cause for the heteronomous control of society and the exploitation of nature and human beings. Private individuals or the state because they hold property should no longer be allowed to exercise power over other human beings, to exploit nature, to command the economy, or to determine the social and political structure of the country. Accordingly, the Greens demanded that the soil, the natural resources, the means of production, and the banks be transferred to a new form of societal property ownership. They reject, however, the well-known demands for ownership by the state since such a system does not allow for participatory controls by the individuals.[120] They favor "self-administered rights of disposition," emphasizing that models for such a system can only be developed by those directly affected. To ensure such self-administration, the means of production and distribution should be decentralized as far as possible into transparent and readily controllable entities. An economic structure of this nature with self-administered units of production and without hierarchical structures must at the same time guarantee that the production decisions are equitable to the social and ecological interests of society as a whole. For this reason, the Greens favor the creation of economic and social councils at all levels as "groups for democratic self-government." They even promise that "in such a social economy there will be no unemployment but rather a just distribution of the work necessitated by society." In supporting the trade union demand for a 35-hour week, they see it as a beginning in a further long-term shortening of the workweek, a step demanding a complete equalization between low and middle incomes. Their program even gives consideration to the idea that income may be available independent of the performance of work; that is, a minimum income may be guaranteed without proof of need so that no one would be forced for purely economic reasons to go to work or be placed into a situation where a choice of work might be imposed.[121]

A few critical comments should be made. The economic program of the Greens fails to include answers to many important questions. Who, for example, would invest if the profit motive were eliminated? It does not address the financing of its own sociopolitical demands. Just one of the suggestions contained in the Green's federal election platform of 1980, namely, that survivor benefits for the widowed should equal the pensions previously paid to the wage earner, would cost an additional DM 20 billion. The reduction of the pension age to 55 would add about DM 30 billion. The Greens fail to answer the question of how they can, on the one hand, demand a continual reduction of government authority in favor of greater individual participation in democracy, but, on the other hand, support additional government social programs that of necessity require an extension of government influence. The demand that those directly affected by such programs create their own organizations seems equally incongruous.

In its federal platform, the Green Party states: "The realization that our existence is dependent primarily on agricultural production—and that this takes precedence over industrial production—is the main principle of Green policy." By this statement, they imply an eventual exit from industrial society into an agricultural idyll.

The chapter on agriculture in the Sindelfingen program is reminiscent of autarkical ideas: "The sufficient and secure supply of healthy food for the population is endangered. In spite of the public discussion of surpluses, there is no certainty of sufficient domestic supply."[122] The welfare of the Federal Republic of Germany is, however, largely based on its industrial potential. The autarky-like ideas of the Greens, which favor a withdrawal from the world's division of labor, would have disastrous consequences for the Federal Republic, for of all the industrialized countries it is the most dependent on international trade: Every fourth worker in the country (5.8 million) lives on exports. Where would the nearly 30 percent of the gross national product

(GNP) now generated by exports originate? Even the beginning of a change toward an alternative economic policy would remove the German economy from the world market. An incidental result would be a considerable economic disadvantage for the developing countries. The economic policy of the Greens is strongly influenced by the Marxist idea of the alienation of the wage earner; the model of a democracy as a council of workers that determines economic and social policies was taken over from earlier times along with the ideas of autarky. In spite of a past in which such ideas were tried and discarded, pronouncements of this nature are attractive to young people because they transmit an image of an attainable utopia, oriented to the desires of self-determination, of an individual's ability to attain specific goals in a lifetime, of the restriction of the anonymous power of the state, and of the assumption by that state of all personal risks.

The Greens and Women's Issues

Ranking immediately after the ecological, alternative, and peace movements, the most important source of Green strength derives from the women's movement. This connection also is the result of the student revolt even though women's issues took on importance that transcended their origin. The student movement provided the base for the first feminist activities. The "revolt of the women" in the Socialist Student Association (SDS), which took place during the final SDS delegates' conference in Hanover in 1968, may be seen as the starting point.[123] In different phases of the women's movement, there arose the beginnings of a feminist counterculture. Although feminist trends exist in other parties and movements, a considerable amount of congruency can be seen between the program of the Greens and that of the women's movement.

The Greens' Women's Program for the European Parliament Elections covers nearly all feminist positions and notes a "widespread use of force against women" in German society. It criticizes the underrepresentation of women in all areas of public life, the sexual discrimination against women and their treatment as objects of male needs, and the reduction of women to the role of mothers. The Greens demand, inter alia, the complete removal of all legal sanctions against the women who have abortions and the doctors who assist them, i.e., the repeal of Paragraph 218 of the German Judicial Code. The 1980 federal program, developed in discussion with the then more influential ecological group, was much more reticent in calling for repeal of this section of the penal code. The Greens' federal program rejects any prosecution for abortion and calls for full health insurance payments to cover its costs. At the same time it points to two goals: the full right of self-determination by women and the right to protect lives—lives already in existence and lives being created.

Among other issues, the Greens demand prosecution for rape, even in marriages. Sexual discrimination against women in the work place is subject to increasingly vehement criticism by the Greens. Former Green Bundestag member Hecker, the chairman of the Committee for Research and Technology, was the subject of accusations concerning sexual misbehavior in the work place. Initially without using his name, three members of the Green office staff prepared a flyer with him as the subject, in which a male member of the Green Bundestag caucus was accused of abusing the prerogatives of a male supervisor in relation to several female staff members. Specifically, he was accused of touching their breasts after having placed a friendly arm around their shoulders during a discussion of the agenda.

The Greens suddenly realized that actions they vehemently rejected in their program could happen among their own members. The rigid moral code of the Greens then led to the decision of the caucus to request the "sexist" Hecker to resign. The moral code of a portion of the caucus made it unable to accept an apology. This moralistic purity empowered the caucus to judge the behavior of its individual members.

From April 3, 1984, to March 30, 1985, the leadership of the Green Bundestag caucus was totally in the hands of women. This was symbolic of the importance of the women's movement in the party. The move was also a tactical maneuver to change the previous leadership and thereby remove Petra Kelly. She criticized the action this way: "They acted just like men. They tricked me. I was not informed. The strategy was, unfortunately, very male."[124] The decision was also sexist because it required that the leadership positions could only be held by women.

As a result of this change, the voters in general were presented with a very feminist profile of the Greens, which may be a useful election move. But in the population as a whole, the development is viewed with a certain amount of skepticism. Of 81 percent who had heard of the change, only 31 percent found it commendable, 47 percent rejected it, and 22 percent were undecided. Among Green voters and younger women, however, approval was higher: Forty-nine percent of the 16- to 19-year-olds approved. Of women who vote Green, 82 percent approved; male Green voters approved by 57 percent.[125]

We Must Get out of NATO

Although the Greens are not identical with the peace movement, they are a part of it and are used by it as its parliamentary arm. The spectrum of the peace movement begins in the left wing of the SPD and includes independents, Greens, and the dogmatic Communists of the DKP. Within the peace movement, the last group persistently tries to prevent any criticism of the Soviet Union and the German Democratic Republic (GDR). Its efforts include the attempted stifling of the swords-into-plowshares slogans of the GDR peace movement that were adopted by portions of the peace movement in the Federal Republic— including the Greens—as a protest against the suppression of the movement in Eastern European countries. Large portions of the peace movement in the Federal Republic demand that Germany withdraw from NATO. At an action conference of the movement in Cologne in May 1984, attended by about 800 people, some voices opposed any immediate withdrawal. According to reports in the Berlin alternative paper *die tageszeitung*, for instance, Wolfgang Biermann, a member of a pro-peace group close to the SPD, stated that a withdrawal from NATO would rob the Federal Republic of the ability to slow the United States in the continued development of its arms program. Such a withdrawal would eliminate the possiblity of throwing a monkey wrench into the U.S. machinery.[126] This part of the peace movement argues in favor of defeating the present government coalition in the next elections to replace it with an SPD-Green coalition and then to fight NATO's plans from within the system.

In their program, the Greens favor the dissolution of both NATO and the Warsaw Pact and conclude "we need to get out of NATO."[127] The demand for a withdrawal from NATO is not unanimous within the Greens. The Duisburg decision, quoted previously, is formulated to be ambiguous, and it permits the interpretation that withdrawal is to be achieved by the dissolution of both military alliances. The Greens demand nuclear free zones and a Europe free of nuclear weapons. They demand some unilateral disarmament by all countries, beginning with the Federal Republic, the withdrawal of all foreign forces,[128] and the reduction of the size of the German Defense Forces. They also seek a mandated work program for conscientious objectors and over the long term the ending of compulsory military service.

A portion of the Greens, or at least its public supporters, favors a nonnuclear defense force for conventional warfare, equipped with defensive weapons only. Ex-General Bastian, a former member of the Green caucus in the Bundestag, presented a two-tiered alternative plan to the Defense Committee of the Bundestag and met considerable resistance among his own party colleagues. The plan's first demand was that atomic, bacterio-logical, and chemical weapons no longer be stored on German soil nor used from it. Germany's position in the Western alliance would then have to be renegotiated. In October 1983, he expressed himself in favor of transforming the army into a militia without mobile or high-technology equipment, of transforming the navy into a coast guard, and of placing the various services under a unified command.

A transition to a second stage could take place when the people had been freed from their fear of threats and when the concept of a weapons-free social defense is practicable. This perception of the second stage was echoed by the majority of his former colleagues. His views of the first stage were quickly put to the test: He was vehemently attacked by his caucus colleagues when he favored the procurement of 200 antitank helicopters, terming them defensive weapons systems. Bahro and many other Greens rejected this view of the ex-general because the Greens were in principle not part of the consensus concerning the Defense Forces. They considered these forces as having been part of NATO from the outset and as having been a way in which the Federal Republic had been drawn into the confrontation between the superpowers, into their arms race, and into their struggle for world domination. Bahro, who generally does not hesitate to enter into controversies with the Soviet bloc, argued that the Soviet Union had less leverage and was concerned with maintaining a hold over Poland and not with seizing West Germany. "The Russians are not coming!"[129] Bahro said and in view of the absence of a Soviet threat favored the Federal Republic unilaterally taking the road to peace and disarmament.

A few critical remarks must be made here. If Bahro was correct in his assumptions, the Greens would have to demand not only the dissolution of NATO and the establishment of nuclear free zones but also the immediate dissolution of the German Federal Defense Forces. The Greens fail to draw this conclusion, however, and instead plead for the right of "total objection to any service" and favor active propagation for conscientious objection and the organization of those granted this right. They also support the complete implementation of civil and trade union rights for all civil servants and military service personnel.[130]

A wide consensus exists among the Greens in their demands "for a defense of the social achievements and for the securing of peace and life by peaceful rather than military means." This goal is to be achieved by a reorientation of the society of the Federal Republic "toward civil courage, resistance, alternative and decentralized structures" so that "it is clear to any aggressive foreign power that any attempt at occupation and domination would cause it more difficulties and burdens than any resultant increase in power would warrant."[131]

The Green Party must, however, face the criticism that its desired defense of the social system without the use of arms would in fact increase the probability of war because it would not be possible to exercise influence against the temptation of a potential enemy to make use of political and military superiority.[132] The Greens must ask themselves whether they are ready to accept any military defense, no matter how structured; they face this problem particularly because a considerable portion of the Greens is either strongly pacifistic or prepared to deny that there is any danger of war being initiated by the Soviet Union.

The pronouncements of the Greens on foreign and security policies and their policy on German reunification are contradictory. The peace manifesto adopted in October 1981 in Offenbach stated that the road to a blocfree Europe requires a "step-by-step withdrawal of the Federal Republic from NATO." It could be assumed that such a view would favor the neutralization of the Federal Republic in a way similar to that existing in Austria. But such a view is never firmly stated. The manifesto also stated: "No German state could ignore an offer by the Federal Republic or the GDR to leave its respective alliance." Does this mean that the Greens favor reunification? In the long run, the defense and security pronouncements of the Greens remain unclear; they do, however, clearly show anti-Americanism. In this connection, former general Bastian criticized an interview given by Jürgen Reents, a former member of the Communist Alliance of Hamburg (later a Z-Group), who had demanded that the West German peace movement maintain its single-minded adversarial attitude toward the United States.[133] Bastian characterized this small minority of the party as one that "favored a policy of unilateral anti-Americanism, which equated the fight against imperialism with a fight against America, which saw only Western imperialism as harmful but glossed over the imperialism of the other superpower."[134] This view, in the opinion of Bastian, is not shared by a majority of the Green voters; they see Green policy as transcending power blocs and advocating neutrality between them, laying equal responsibility on both superpowers and seeking to bring about disarmament by both.

Although the Soviet Union is occasionally criticized, the decisions of the Greens in foreign and security policy give rise to the assumption by the Greens that the United States had adopted an offensive war plan and was potentially the power that would strike first. At best the Greens took a position equidistant from both superpowers, not recognizing that the United States is founded on democratic principles. When a Green delegation visited Moscow in October 1983 at the invitation of the Soviet government, Manon Maren-Grisebach, a member of the party executive, declared that the desire for peace and the readiness to negotiate an agreement in Geneva on intermediate-range ballistic missiles were more believable in Moscow than in Washington.[135] Even though the Greens' trip to Moscow was poorly planned, they did not become ready ambassadors of Moscow's policies. They pointed out the violation of human rights while they were in Moscow and conducted a minidemonstration on Red Square, which, however, was hardly noticed. Quarrels within the caucus had led to an absence of substantive agreement among the delegation members. In her report, Petra Kelly wrote that it had not been possible before the departure of the delegation to hold the necessary substantive discussions to enable the delegation to travel with a clear negotiating plan. This situation was unfortunate because members of the delegation held differing views on the demands for disarmament to be presented in Moscow. The delegation members had hurriedly agreed upon a negotiating position on the night prior to their departure—a situation that she had found totally inadequate.[136]

6
THE GREENS AND THE SPD

One of the most important issues of Green policy is the relationship of the party to the traditional parties and especially to the SPD. The party has had little contact with the Christian Union parties. As stated earlier, the fundamental oppositionist and radical ecologist factions of the Green Party always warned of the dangers of too close a collaboration with the SPD. Bahro vehemently opposed such a tie because he felt that the Greens also needed to appeal to more conservative and Christian Union voters. Trampert, the spokesman for the party executive, opposed this view and spoke out against any suggestion of a relationship between the Greens and the CDU.[137] Only a vanishing minority believes such a cooperative effort to be possible.[138]

On the other hand, the Greens have had numerous contacts with the SPD during their short history. A book by Joschka Fischer that appeared a few weeks prior to the 1983 elections stated: "Perhaps the Greens are merely a pocket-sized version of the Independent Socialdemocratic Party of Germany [a splinter group that left the mainstream Socialist movement in 1917 but recombined with it in 1922 to form the Social Democratic Party of Germany] and that old lady 'Social Democracy' is once more in one of the crises of her life."[139] Clearly, in the view of many Greens, a minimal consensus with the SPD does exist, a consensus reflecting common ideas and a common politicoideological tradition. Not only has the political proximity between the parties led to a special relationship—the left wing of the SPD considers itself part of the peace movement—but in two states specific possibilities of cooperation have already arisen. Even though negotiations about cooperation in Hamburg failed in 1982, long and difficult negotiations led in 1984 to the reelection of SPD Minister President Börner in Hessen. This reelection was only possible with Green support, and the subsequent passage of a state budget could only be enacted with deliberate Green abstention. The decision to provide a measure of Green support to the minority government in Hessen was not reached without considerable debate within the Green Party. The opposition was led by a fundamentalist group calling itself radical ecologists. But this group remained a distinct minority even though it was supported by the federal executive of the party, particularly Trampert. Moreover, the attempt to impose the view held at the federal level on the state party tended to have counterproductive consequences. Trampert defended the decision of the federal executive in an eight-page statement read at the convention of the Hessen Green Party. In it he said: "We want to prevent that the Greens are put in a position where they exist solely as a junior partner of the SPD, a role which might assure the creation of majorities and put the CDU into the opposition but which otherwise places the Greens into a subordinate role in the formulation of policy."[140] The earlier criticism of the Hamburg Greens, which had been directed especially at Trampert, was now aimed at the negotiations in Hessen, where the preparation for the negotiations was criticized as "being conducted in a dilettante manner."[141]

Equally vehement differences arose within the Greens' federal caucus about the alliance in Hessen. Petra Kelly, herself formerly a member of the SPD, opposed this type of cooperation, as did Bahro. In a March 1984 caucus report she regretted that steps were taken "without prior dicussion, in which the Greens made themselves available as future junior partners of the SPD." The SPD was described as a party with "a bit of defense force, a bit of pacifism, a bit of adherence to the NATO alliance and a bit of neutralism"—a party which in spite of its continued relationship to NATO also wanted to play a leading role in the peace movement that rejects NATO.[142]

Petra Kelly's criticism was directed primarily at Otto Schily, her colleague in the Greens' Bundestag caucus. On August 11, 1983, he had voiced the view that the Greens should seek a sufficiently high percentage of the votes to enable the party to become the junior coalition partner in a future government and indicated he was looking for the formation of such a coalition with the SPD.[143] In spite of the criticism that he drew from within the party for his junior-partner phraseology, he continued to speak out for cooperation with the SPD because he saw the need for a coalition partnership if the Greens were to realize specific political goals.[144] In various interviews he made clear that his party should at some time be able to participate directly in a government.[145]

Among SPD voters, a readiness for a coalition with the Greens seems to be increasing. The research organization Forschungsgruppe Wahlen Mannheim conducted a survey in Hessen on September 26, 1983 (prior to the 1983 Hessen elections) and found that 25 percent of the SPD voters and approximately 80 percent of the Green voters favored cooperation between the two parties in Hessen should the election results make it impossible for any one party alone to form a government. In a nationwide survey two months later, 45 percent of the SPD voters and nearly 90 percent of the Green voters favored SPD-Green cooperation in Hessen.[146] This same survey also showed that SPD voters still harbored strong reservations against an alliance with the Greens, a fact not calculated to make life easier for SPD politicians.

In analysis of the voting pattern for the federal executive of the SPD, the dilemma of this party's relationship to the Greens again became apparent. These voters had considerable sympathy for the Greens (29 percent list the Greens as their second choice), but about half of these voters (51 percent) list them as their fourth (last) choice. On the other hand, 43 percent of these voters list the CDU/CSU as their second choice, but only 24 percent as their last.[147] Of the Green voters, 81 percent list the SPD as their second choice. This result indicates the limitation placed on the Greens in seeking a possible coalition partner. The SPD, on the other hand, faces a dilemma because any coalition it might seek would be unpopular with a considerable portion of its voters.

If it did not do so earlier, the SPD must have given considerable thought after the March 1983 federal elections to how it might recapture some of the Green votes since the electoral gains of this new party were achieved primarily at the SPD's expense. This voter realignment was documented in three Baden-Württemberg legislative districts in which the Greens had failed to submit their list of candidates before the filing deadline. As a result no Greens were on the ballot, and the SPD gained voters with an election result of 5:1:1 in relation to the CDU and FDP, respectively. In this same election, the Greens showed a marked increase in voting strength in all remaining districts.

The general identity of the potential Green voters with those of the SPD was also confirmed by the election statistics published by the Federal Office of Statistics in Wiesbaden. As indicated earlier, all German voters have two votes, one for the direct election of the local candidate and a second, perhaps more important, for the party of their choice. The candidate for the local election district is elected by direct majority vote; the party votes are allotted by a system of proportional representation. In the direct elections, only the candidates of the two major parties have a chance of being elected. The division of the second votes becomes interesting, therefore, because it indicates which voters might have voted Green on the second ballot and which party's candidate these voters preferred on the first ballot. Of 1,000 second ballot votes for the Greens in the 1983 elections (1980 figures in parentheses), the SPD had received 398 (187) first ballot votes; the CDU, 43 (70); the CSU, 9 (48); the FDP 12, (14); and the Green candidates themselves, 521 (649). Every second Green voter, therefore, had given the first vote to another party, with 39.8 percent of the Green voters preferring the SPD, only 4.3 percent the CDU, 0.9 percent the CSU, and 1.2 percent the FDP. This breakdown shows a much closer affinity of the Green voters to the SPD than to any of the other traditional parties.[148]

Not only the SPD itself but also its official youth group, the Young Socialists (Jusos), are thus targeted by the existence of the Greens. As late as the early 1970's the Young Socialists were close to the protest movement and were able to integrate some protesting young people into the SPD. Later, many of the young people involved in the protest scene no longer joined the Young Socialists but instead became members of the Greens. As a result, the Jusos are now unable to create much interest within the younger generation. In the immediate future this must have a devastating effect on the SPD because German parties always look to their youth organizations for new blood.[149]

The effort by the left wing of the SPD to draw Green supporters into its own ranks was also demonstrated by the invitation of SPD Bundestag member Erhard Eppler to Gert Bastian to join the SPD after he had left the Green caucus. "I would be pleased to be able to work together with Bastian in the SPD," he said. Bastian could join the SPD and plead his ideas there; there are those in the SPD whose ideas on questions of arms and peace are considerably more radical than Bastian's, Epple added.[150]

The elections to the legislatures in Berlin and the Saarland on March 10, 1985, are of special importance to the future relationship between the Greens and the SPD. The SPD leader in Berlin was former Defense Minster Hans Apel who belongs to the right wing of the SPD and who had rigorously rejected any cooperation with the Greens. The SPD obtained only 32.4 percent of the votes, a loss of 5.9 percent from the previous (1981) elections. The Berlin Alternative List (AL), a close affiliate of the federal Green Party, gained votes from 7.2 percent in 1981 to 10.6 percent in 1985. This result favoring the AL may in part be traced to the social structure existing in the city of Berlin (a metropolis with a high proportion of students and of employment in the service industries). Polls taken prior to the elections gave the AL an even higher percentage of the votes.

In the Saarland, on the other hand, the SPD standard bearer was Oskar Lafontaine, who was acceptable to the younger voters of the Saarland not only because of his own youthfulness but also because he is an active adherent of the peace movement. At a number of rallies he had spoken in opposition to the NATO rearmament decision. Moreover, his fellow candidate, slated for the post of minister for environmental affairs, was Jo Leinen, an important member of the ecological movement. Leinen had for many years chaired the Federal Association of Citizen Initiatives for the Protection of the Environment (BBU) and had actively campaigned against the NATO rearmament program. The two candidates were, therefore, not only more acceptable to the Saarland's Green voters, but Lafontaine had been able to recruit Green voters by the conditions he laid before the Saarland's Green Party. Lafontaine categorically rejected the coalition-by-tolerance structure of government that pertains in Hessen where an SPD minority government rules by Green sufferance. He made it clear that the stated refusal by the Greens to join any future governing coalition made it essential that the SPD receive a clear majority. Obviously, many Green voters did not share their leadership's view about not becoming coalition partners. Moreover, the sociostructural situation in the Saarland is less favorable to the Greens than elsewhere (a largely Catholic population, which tends to give the Greens fewer votes than the Protestants, and so on).

The initial reaction within the Green Party laid the defeat to the refusal to join a coalition government and to Lafontaine's personal charisma. It also noted that Lafontaine had been able to suggest to the Green voters that a vote for the Greens would result in a CDU government. The results in the Saarland should, however, strengthen those in the Green Party who favor mid- or long-term cooperation with the SPD or at least its left wing.

The SPD's success in the May 12, 1985, elections in North-rhine-Westphalia, in which it achieved an absolute majority, was to some extent at the expense of the Greens. Even though the Greens increased their voter share by 1.6 percent, they failed to overcome the 5 percent minimum required for representation. Because this state has a large labor population, the Greens were traditionally weak there; moreover, many potential Green voters may have chosen to vote for the SPD because of internal squabbles within the Green Party. Following the election, the debate within the Green Party again focused on the question of the relationship to the SPD—should it differentiate itself more thoroughly or seek closer cooperation. The conclusion drawn is bound also to affect the programmatic cooperation existing between the two parties in Hessen.

7
THE RELATIONSHIP
OF THE GREENS
TO COMMUNIST GROUPS

Although the German Communist Party (DKP) and its functionaries repeatedly offered the Greens a coalition partnership, in actual fact the relationship between the two parties has been rather cool. The Greens know that any publicly visible cooperation with a Moscow-directed Communist group would harm their image with the German population. Adherents of the Greens, therefore, took pains to differentiate themselves from the Communists in the peace movement by supporting the concept of swords-into-plowshares, which was opposed by Moscow. At the time of the elections to the European Parliament, there appeared a separate "peace list" under DKP influence.

At the same time the Greens warned against any attempt to avoid all coincidental identity of objectives, since a primary goal of the Greens remained the prevention of the implementation of the NATO decision on rearmament. At various times, many Greens cooperated with DKP members in so-called action committees. The argument that anyone cooperating with opponents of democracy served to make such opponents socially acceptable was countered by the view that all "progressive" forces had to work together to defeat such policies as the NATO rearmament decision.

During the initial phase of their existence, the Greens profited from the collapse of various Marxist-Leninist groups, especially in those city-states in which the party participated in local elections through so-called alternative lists, namely, in Hamburg and Berlin. In this period, the German Ministry of Interior estimated that about a quarter of the members and candidates of the Alternative Lists had previously belonged to the Maoist Communist Party of Germany (KPD).[151]

At the time that Gert Bastian threatened to leave the Green Party, he wrote to the party executive that the party and its caucus in the Bundestag "consistently advanced forces which had begun to alter the goals and content of Green policy in a way that was no longer defensible" and then specifically took issue with the Z-Group.

> The initial errors in the political development of the Greens became especially apparent in the success of the former Z-Group which had originated in the Communist Alliance. It began to occupy key positions in Party councils and jointly with former or newly-found ideological colleagues succeeded in outvoting the unorganized majority of those with differing views, both in the caucus and in the regional organizations, using skillful and disciplined cadre techniques.[152]

One Z-Group member, Rainer Trampert, was elected as one of three speakers of the federal executive at the party's federal convention on November 12–14, 1982. In the view of people at the Institute for Marxist Studies and Research (IMSF), an organization close to the DKP, the Z-Group is in fact the organizational backbone of the Hamburg Greens.[153] It is a splinter group of the Communist Alliance, which exercised a certain amount of influence in northern Germany and unequivocally represents Marxist-Leninist positions. The split was primarily over the issue of active participation in the formation of the

Green Party. In early 1982, the Z-Group furnished six of the eight members of the Hamburg Green Party's executive council.[154]

At that time, the spokesman for the Green-Alternative List (GAL), Thomas Ebermann, was also a member of the Z-Group. At the time of the split, he favored forming a voting bloc to increase the influence of the Greens;[155] in an August 1982 interview as chairman of the GAL caucus in Hamburg, he stated that the Z-Group's policy would continue to be adherence to the principle of separate Marxist organizations.[156] The Z-Group continued in existence and exercised its influence on party and caucus in part because it had its own means of communication— the newsletter *Moderne Zeiten*. The Green caucus in the Bundestag includes individuals who work with the organizations of the extreme Left, such as the journalist Jürgen Reents (formerly of the Communist Alliance, now a member of the Z-Group) and Dr. Sabine Bard, who in the years from 1973 to 1979 participated in events in Augsburg and Munich sponsored by the former KPD and the League against Imperialism. This does not mean that former members of Communist organizations should not have the right to change their views. But it must be assumed that these former activists in Marxist-Leninist groups are moving the Greens toward a leftist socialist party; they believe that fractionalized isolation into separate splinter groups can only lead to political failure.

8
THE GREENS: POWER OR NUISANCE?

The Greens pose a challenge to the traditional parties; they have become a factor in German politics and according to their own frequent statements (particularly those by Joschka Fischer)[157] believe themselves to be a political power to be reckoned with. They will probably not disappear quickly as had been assumed in a number of commentaries after they first entered the Bundestag in 1983. Ever since the "Generation of '68," there has been a protest movement of some sort in the Federal Republic. The movement was often said to be dead, but in fact it eventually created the basis for the Greens' electoral successes. In many ways, the Greens have become an important factor in German politics and are increasingly in the process of leaving the characteristics of a movement and taking on those of a political party.

1. Even though the Greens frequently refer to themselves as a "party of the movement" and many of their members still cling to the mystique surrounding a "movement," the Greens have in fact for some time assumed the characteristics of a party. They are both: movement and party. A movement has a general political orientation and direction but frequently has no clearly defined, comprehensive program. A number of political ideologies interconnect its members. It is also characteristic of a movement that its members do not need to be formally organized

and that it rests on the shoulders of an increasing number of activists. The end of a social movement as a continuing force of protest occurs, for example, when as a political party it is fully integrated into the political system,[158] when its demands, which were previously sharply differentiated from the accepted social norm, have been incorporated into the general culture of the society; or when the movement has recognized that the goals envisioned by it for society can be achieved only as a part of a long-term social development.[159]

In a formal sense, that is, with regard to organization, apparatus, and leadership structure, the Greens have already become a party, particularly since they have accepted the law governing political parties by their participation in elections. They have increasingly become participants in the parliamentary process, forcing the party to take detailed positions on nearly all political issues. On the other hand, the Greens continue to fight against playing a parliamentary role and against being a party. "Without the extra-parliamentary movement, a small parliamentary caucus such as ours would be completely powerless."[160] At the moment, the Greens are not ready to accept the responsibility of governing. At best they tolerate minority governments led by the SPD. It is characteristic of movements that they represent particular interests, whereas a readiness to assume responsibility of government includes the readiness to accept responsibility for all. The fear of integration into the existing political system is at present still greater than the readiness to assume joint responsibility within the framework of the existing political order.

The discussion about the Green Party's character as a movement found great resonance during the party's seventh regular convention, which took place in Hamburg, December 7–9, 1984, when Rudolf Bahro, who left the party's executive at that time, declared: "Formally and structurally, movement, state and society confront each other similarly to the way they did in the Weimar Republic. The Greens are rising in form—and in form only—in a way similar to the rise of the Nazi Party."[161] This accusation was nearly unanimously rejected, and the convention passed a resolution condemning any endorsement of this view. The convention recognized the major harm that such a statement could cause. Any use of this statement to link the Greens to the Nazis would bring about serious problems for the Greens, even though the two movements may have relied on similar antiparliamentary and anti-Western attitudes. Moreover, the Green Party has not endorsed the principle of a *Führer*, a principle that was an essential ingredient in both fascism and National Socialism.

Among Greens, opposition to specific attitudes of German society remains a connecting element. Nevertheless, they have been increasingly required to define their own role and to state positive political positions. Of course, this does not exclude the splintering of parties or the formation of wings as is true in other parties.

Whether the Greens are solely a movement or are also a party must also be examined by looking at their means of communication. The party has established its own communications network, using information services and magazines, and has taken advantage of the manifold opportunites offered by modern mass media, such as radio and television, for the presentation of its policies. Although in the early days the Green movement used the broad spectrum of the alternative press as the most important instrument for the presentation of its policies, Green positions are now also made known through established media.

2. A further indication that the Greens are becoming a political party is the fact that they have been able to develop a relatively stable group of potential voters. This has enabled them to create regional organizations drawing on federal financial support for reimbursement of their campaign expenditures. Nearly 70 percent of the Green voters are under 35 years old, giving the party a youthful profile. Analyses of voter composition show that the Greens are drawing on a repeat-voter potential—the percentage of voters who previously voted Green is growing. More than

half of those who voted Green in 1984 had voted for the party before. Although an initial vote for a party is significant for future elections, a second or third vote for the same party shows an extraordinary firming of voter adherence. It may be assumed, therefore, that the Greens will be able to continue to draw on a stable voter base.

3. The Greens have been elected primarily because their style and program are different from that of the other parties. This became especially clear in the elections for the Baden-Württenberg legislature in March 1984, one year after the Greens entered the Bundestag. Prior to the elections, the entire Green caucus was rotated; Wolf-Dieter Hasenclever, a national figure, rejected the idea of rotation and therefore refused to be a candidate; and the state party convention was chaotic and publicly displayed the considerable differences within it. In spite of these factors, the party registered considerable gains. All other parties, on the other hand, would have had to assume that this type of internal dissent would be likely to reduce their voter support.

The Greens give the impression in their platforms of a diverse attitude of protest, reflecting a mixture of conservative criticism of society on the one hand and traditional criticism of capitalism on the other. The party thereby appeals to a wide spectrum of the dissatisfied. It continues to attract young people by the unorthodox outward appearance of its members.

4. The fear of contact that many of the Greens have in relation to democratic institutions, and particularly of any integration into a society of which it is critical in principle, will fade the longer those Greens who are elected can exercise some power, even if only as representatives of the opposition. The Greens, perhaps without desiring it, fulfill a political function by providing a focal point for those who feel the need to protest; their support of the Greens focuses their political will. This integrating process of the dissatisfied lends support to the view held by protest groups that, at least for a midrange period, political minorities can organize effectively in a democratic

society. This should not be read as minimizing the danger of a number of antiparliamentary tendencies within the Green movement.

5. Even if an overwhelming majority of the Green voters desires to support the SPD-led government in Hessen—a support temporarily interrupted by differences over two nuclear power stations—the Greens know that a traditional coalition is likely to be anathema to some of their own voters. They continue to view the party caucus as the "parliamentary arm of various minorities, minor movements and subcultures and supported by the counter-culture."[162] Joschka Fischer recommended, therefore, that the Greens be both a power factor and a nuisance factor. They will retain their identity as long as they feel that they are part of the counterculture. They must, therefore, opppose the idea of integration in relationship to their own members while simultaneously attempting to use parliament for the presentation of the ideas of the new social movement. This difficult balancing act between an acceptance of parliamentary democracy and the resulting political integration into the system, on the one hand, and the identification with a new social movement, on the other, will determine how long the Greens will continue to exist.

6. The longer the Greens remain in parliamentary bodies, the more they will be faced with the necessity of developing specific ideas for programs that are not solely negative. The fractionalization that may result from such a requirement, some of which is already noticeable, could lead to a reduction in the party's ability to integrate various points of view. At this moment, it is primarily success itself that holds the party together.[163] The tendencies within the Green Party to develop into a left-wing socialist party will continue to increase even though the recipe for its success lies in its ability to represent the broad spectrum of protest movements. A serious power struggle is developing between the various wings in both the party and its Bundestag caucus, and it seems to be strengthening the left-wing socialist

segment. The members of the caucus themselves hold such divergent views that the group has been unable to develop into a party power center even though its members are the party's key figures. The manner in which the party conventions have dealt with the reports of the Bundestag members indicates a degree of aversion against the caucus unimaginable in other parties. The Hamburg ecosocialists and Z-Group in particular were able to prevent the Bundestag members from exercising any dominating influence over the decisions of the party. Trampert and Ebermann continue to favor the principles of rotation and the imposed mandate, presumably because they hope thereby to obtain more control over the caucus after the 1987 elections.

7. It may be assumed that in the 1987 Bundestag elections, the Greens will again exceed the 5 percent minimum and continue to send representatives to the Bundestag. But it would be too early for the Greens to be confident about such an outcome. Their campaign strategy will not be made easier by the fact that they surpassed the 5 percent barrier in 1983 by only a fraction of a percentage point. Although in the elections to the European parliament in 1984 and in subsequent state legislative elections (with the exception of that in the Saarland in March 1985) they were able to stabilize and consolidate their following, it must be borne in mind that by providing their adherents with a base for protest in these regional elections it was easier for the Greens than for the traditional parties to mobilize their voters. Elections to the state legislatures, and perhaps even elections to the European parliament, tend to be used by the voters to express their opposition to the governing coalition in Bonn. Additionally, some voters may be more ready to register their opposition by voting for a protest party in the "less important" state and communal elections than in "decisive" Bundestag elections. Voter turnout in these elections is usually 20 percent lower than in the federal elections, a factor likely to have a negative effect on the parties represented in the federal government. Moreover, the Greens' substantial election gains were tempered by their first

defeats in the elections to the legislatures in the Saarland on March 10, 1985, in which they received only 2.5 percent of the votes and in Northrhine-Westphalia where with 4.6 percent of the votes they were unable to gain any seats. Much will depend on the way the Greens act in the Bundestag. During their first year of parliamentary representation, they were able to present their goals in parliamentary debates, press conferences, and television interviews with skill and effectiveness. The initial caucus leadership, however, was made up of a number of prominent Greens who have since been replaced in their leadership roles.

The probability of a successful reelection of the Green Party members is also supported by the fact that a considerable number of its voters have an anti-institutional bias that is also directed at the party itself. These voters support the rotation principle and interpret a certain amount of chaos within the party as creative achievement.

8. The probability that Green Party members will succeed in being reelected in 1987 is also supported by the fact that the majority of the German population—52 percent—see the representation of the Greens in the Bundestag as a positive development; this figure is made up of 62 percent SPD adherents, 45 percent FDP, and 35 percent from the Christian Union parties.[164] The Greens, therefore, are not seen as a party outside the acceptable political framework, which had been true in the case of previously constituted small political parties that had failed to pass the 5 percent minimum vote requirement. This generally friendly acceptance by the population does, of course, support the idea of the Greens as a factor in domestic politics. Even political opponents of the Greens have voiced the view that the Green Party could be useful in regenerating the vitality of parliaments and in removing the encrusted structures. According to a 1984 survey, the Greens have a voter potential of approximately 9 percent—a potential that they have not yet fully exploited.[165]

9. Of the traditional parties, the SPD is directly affected by the existence of the Greens, as is the FDP, which has to fear for its continued existence as a parliamentary party. The Christian Union parties are affected less than the others. The ability of the SPD to integrate protest movements into the party was sharply curtailed by the policies of former Chancellor Helmut Schmidt. As a result, the efforts of the Young Socialists to act as a bridgehead to the extraparliamentary opposition[166] increasingly lacked success. The experience in Hessen, where the SPD was able to govern as a minority government by Green toleration, shows that the Greens may well become crucial in forming a coalition, a situation already reality in some communal councils. Even though the idea is only rarely voiced, it is unquestionably true that some Green party politicians dream of taking over the role played in the past by the FDP in being the crucial element in the formation of German governments. This idea was voiced by former SDS leader Cohn-Bendit: "If the Greens want to continue to influence policy and to rattle the power relationships within the parliamentary institutions of the Federal Republic, then the party must face up to the issue of participation in a coalition."[167]

In the SPD, too, thought is being given to this possibility. The SPD leader in the Saarland, Oskar Lafontaine, speaking before his clear majority victory in the March 1985 elections, thought a red-Green coalition possible, depending on the election results and the willingness of the Greens to work with the SPD in a coalition.[168]

But the situation is disastrous for the SPD. If its left wing seeks an opening to the Greens (such as a repudiation of the previously accepted NATO rearmament decision), it could make an SPD-Green coalition more likely. But such a move would solidify the Green voter potential and thereby limit the SPD to approximately 40 percent of the total vote. Many of the Green voters who might otherwise look to the SPD will be confirmed in their decision to vote Green if they see the two parties cooperating. They would also assume that such a coalition would be most likely to bring about change. On the other hand, the SPD must fear the loss of those voters who are skeptical about a cooperative venture with the Greens. All this confirms that the Greens have become a factor on the landscape of German politics.

10. The future of the Green Party can only be understood if it is not seen as a temporary phenomenon. Its success resulted from the development of the student revolt of 1968 into a protest movement that has continued to grow. The causes of protest frequently remained unchanged; only rarely have political consequences been considered. Demands center on a political-ideological confrontation, stemming especially from the Greens' distinctive concept of democracy. In various policy statements, this party has questioned the concept of representative democracy incorporated in the Basic Law and has instead propagated utopian ideas of a democracy of local councils based on ideas of worker self-government.

An important part of the political interaction engendered by the Greens remains focused on ecological issues—in this area they deserve credit for some accomplishments although both the federal and state governments have recently made important decisions in this area. The key in the debate with the Greens centers on the role of parliament and its freely elected members and the appreciation of the role of law in the resolution of conflicts. The Greens have found special resonance among the young because they placed thoughtful issues at the center of their policy.

The challenge of the Greens requires an examination of the historical ideological tradition in which this movement exists. The University of Bonn political scientist Karl-Dietrich Bracher developed the capsulized description "criticism of civilization, cultural pessimism and anti-capitalism"[169] and has drawn parallels between the Greens and both right-wing and left-wing antidemocratic movements during the Weimar Republic, which

had similar anti-Western traditions. Because the Greens continued the tradition of antiliberalism, antiparliamentarism, and
anticapitalism he termed them "a left-right phenomenon of
protest ideology."

The longing for utopia that so frequently exists in the younger
generation, the search for complete explanations and definitive
answers—these phenomena explain the success of the Greens;
romantic ideas can easily lead to an abjuring of world ills. But
the debate with the Greens cannot overlook their populist base,
especially on ecological issues, where they frequently try to
convey the impression that they possess sacred ideas that will
rescue humanity from the apocalypse. The doctrine of salvation
embodied in the issue of ecology is only an outline, however,
of the vision for a future society. Many of the ideas of the
Greens result from their discomfort with the modern world.
Because of this, they increasingly question the ties of the Federal
Republic to the Western world. The neutralism and pacifism of
many Greens could easily to lead to a resurgent nationalism.[170]

NOTES

1. For details, see Gerd Langguth, *Protestbewegung, Entwicklung, Niedergang, Renaissance—Die Neue Linke seit 1968*, Cologne 1983, pp. 24–46.

2. Ludwig von Friedeburg, *Jugend in der modernen Gesellschaft*, Cologne-Berlin 1965, p. 18.

3. Richard Löwenthal, *Der romantische Rückfall*, Stuttgart 1970, p. 13.

4. Jürgen Haberman, *Protestbewegung und Hochschulreform*, Frankfurt 1969, p. 192.

5. It must be emphasized that the roots of the Green Party do not lie in terrorism even though a few former terrorists after renouncing their adherence to that doctrine are now actively involved with the Greens. But in the early 1970's terrorism was an important factor, and its practitioners claimed the SDS as their base.

6. Herbert Gruhl, *Ein Planet wird geplündert—Die Schreckensbilanz unserer Politik*, Frankfurt 1975.

7. For details, see Joseph Huber, *Wer soll das alles ändern*, Berlin 1981.

8. For details, see Claudia Mast, *Aufbruch ins Paradies*, Zurich 1981.

9. Jürgen Bacia and Klaus-Jürgen Scherer, *Passt blos auf! Was will die neue Jugendbewegung*, Berlin 1981, p. 10.

10. Ibid, p. 21.

11. See also Huber, op. cit; Langguth, op. cit, pp. 250ff.

12. Survey by the Institut für Demoskopie, Allensbach, ms., March 5, 1982.

13. Cf. Wolfgang Rüdig, "Bürgerinitiativen im Umweltschutz," in

Hauff (ed.), *Buergerinitiativen in der Gesellschaft,* Villingen-Schwenningen 1980, pp. 133ff.

14. Heidrun Abromeit, "Parteiverdrossenheit und Alternativbewegung," in *Politische Vierteljahresschrift (PVS),* Issue 2, July 1982, p. 181.

15. Flyer of the BBU entitled "Selbstverständnis der Bürgerinitiativen," undated.

16. Cf. Carl Beddermann, "Die Grüne Liste Umweltschutz in Niedersachsen," in Rudolf Brun (ed.), *Der grüne Protest—Herausforderung durch die Umweltsparteien,* Frankfurt 1978.

17. Ibid., p. 111.

18. *radikal* 40, May 26–June 9, 1978, p. 3.

19. Regarding his ideology, see Langguth, op. cit., pp. 114–121.

20. Holger Strohm, "Warum die Bunten bunt sind," in Brun, op. cit., pp. 134ff.

21. Ibid., p. 130.

22. In the two city elections in Hamburg on July 6, 1982, and December 19, 1982, there were no competing groups. There was only the GAL, which received 7.7 percent of the votes and nine seats in the first election and 6.8 percent and eight seats in the second. The second election became necessary because the SPD lost its absolute majority in the first election and the FDP failed to gain any seats. Unless it entered a grand coalition with the CDU, the SPD was dependent on a "coalition of toleration" with the GAL. When this proved impossible, new elections were called.

23. Langguth, op. cit., p. 264.

24. *Innere Sicherheit,* Issue 48, May 18, 1979.

25. The GLU initially affiliated with the GLH, then withdrew in light of the influence of the New Left, especially the Maoist KPD. On July 23, 1978, the GLU Executive decided on a merger with the GLH that was, however, not approved by all the members and led to a further split.

26. Richard Stöss, "Aktionsgemeinschaft Unabhängiger Deutscher," in Richard Stöss (ed.), *Parteienhandbuch—die Parteien der Bundesrepublik Deutschland 1945–1980,* Vol. 1, p. 315.

27. Claus D. Troitsch, "Die Herausforderung der 'etablierten' Parteien durch die Grünen," in Heino Kaack and Reinhold Roth (ed.), *Handbuch des deutschen Parteiensytems,* 1980, Vol 1, p. 273.

28. *die tageszeitung,* January 15, 1980.

29. *Die Zeit,* January 19, 1980.

30. Ibid.

31. Cf. Erwin Teufel, "Die Grünen—Zwischen Bewegung und Partei," in *Sonde,* Issue 3, 1982.

32. *die tageszeitung,* March 24, 1980; see also *Frankfurter Rundschau,* same date.

33. Ibid.

34. Jens Fischer, "Vom Braunen zum Grünen," in *Vorwärts,* April 17, 1980. Cf. also Herbert Riehl-Heyse, "August Haussleiter—viele Fahnen getragen," in *Süddeutsche Zeitung,* April 3, 1980; Michael Schwelin, "Die fünfte Partei des 75-jährigen—Eine Welle, die jeden umschmeisst," in *Stuttgarter Zeitung,* April 15, 1980.

35. *die tageszeitung,* November 3, 1982; cf. also *Frankfurter Allgemeine Zeitung,* November 15, 1982.

36. *Die Welt,* March 6, 1984.

37. Ibid. A vehement intraparty confrontation arose when the Berlin delegate Michael Klöckner demanded autonomous status in Strasbourg. He had left the Green delegate group in October 1984 to preserve his political and financial independence. He claimed never to have made a secret of the fact that he was not a member of the Green Party. On November 3–4, 1984, he used the meeting of the Executive Committee of the Greens to criticize the party for "taking activists and using them to warm chairs as functionaries" (*Süddeutsche Zeitung,* November 5, 1984). He refused to share his office funds with other members of the Green caucus but planned to transfer them to his Berlin group. The Greens finally withdrew all office support funds. (Cf. *Frankfurter Rundschau,* November 5, 1984.)

38. *die tageszeitung,* July 3, 1984.

39. Ibid., July 14, 1984.

40. Ibid.; cf. also West-German Radio Interview, July 13, 1984.

41. Resolution on the Attitude of the Greens in Relation to the Traditional Parties, Minutes of the Seventh Federal Assembly of the Green Party, *Grüner Basis-Dienst,* Issue 1/85, p. 46.

42. Cf. Wilhelm E. Bürklin, "Die Grünen und die neue Politik," in *PVS,* Issue 4, December 1981, p. 359.

43. Cf. Christian Graf von Krockow, "Grenzen der Politik," in *Aus Politik und Zeitgeschichte,* B32–33/82, August 14, 1982.

44. Cf. especially Ronald Inglehart, *The Silent Revolution*, Princeton 1977.

45. For details concerning the change in values, see Gerd Langguth, *Jugend ist anders*, Freiburg-Basel-Vienna, pp. 25ff.

46. Claus Offe, "Konkurrenzpartei und kollektive politische Identität," in Ronald Roth (ed.), *Parliamentarisches Ritual und politische Alternativen*, Frankfurt and New York 1980, pp. 30ff.

47. This is an Alternative List affiliated with the federal Green Party, even though there may also be a statewide Green Party organization.

48. The results of the research by the Federal Statistical Office were published, inter alia, in *Frankfurter Allgemeine Zeitung*, September 1, 1983.

49. The research of the Social Studies Research Institute of the Konrad-Adenauer-Stiftung were made available by its director, Dr. Hans-Joachim Veen. Cf. also Veen, "Wer wählt grün?" in *Aus Politik und Zeitgeschichte*, B35–36/84.

50. "Frequent" attendance at church services: 31 percent CDU/CSU adherents, 13 per cent FDP, 8 percent SPD, and 18 percent of the total population.

51. Jugendwerk der deutschen Shell, *Jugend 81*, Hamburg 1981, Vol. 1, pp. 689f.

52. According to an analysis by Zweites Deutsches Fernsehen, "Bonner Perspektiven," October 21, 1984.

53. See also *Stern*, Issue 36/1984, and *Handelsblatt*, July 5, 1984.

54. See *Bundestagsdrucksache 10/2172*, October 23, 1984. (Publication of the 1983 Accounts of the Political Parties—An Information by the President of the Bundestag.)

55. Stephan Eisel, "Reichste der Parteien," in *Sonde*, Issue 4–84/1–85, p. 63. Amounts based on income without regard to loans.

56. Ibid.

57. Die Grünen im Bundestag (ed.), *Bericht zur Lage der Fraktion*, Bonn, March 1984, p. 5.

58. Ibid., p. 15.

59. *Grüner Basis-Dienst*, Issue 2, 1984.

60. Emil Peter Müller, *Soziale Strukturen im X. Deutschen Bundestag*, Cologne 1983. The data concerning employment are taken from a valuable analysis by Helmut Fogt, "Die Grünen in den Parlamenten

der Bundesrepublik," in *Zeitschrift für Parlamentsfragen,* Issue 4, December 1983, pp. 500ff.

61. The founding document was published, inter alia, in *Gürner Basis-Dienst,* Issue 3/84, pp. 21ff, which also carried criticism of the document. See also Michael Stamm, "Die Gründungserklärung der 'Oekolibertären Grünen': Avantgardismus im Namen der 'schweigenden Mehrheit,'" in *Moderne Zeiten,* Issue 4, April 1984, pp. 12ff; also the position paper "Wider die Lust am Untergang," which was adopted on January 5–6, 1984, in Bad Soden and which preceded the founding declaration, published in *Grüner Basis-Dienst,* Issue 1, January 1984, pp. 10ff.

62. *die tageszeitung,* November 3, 1982.

63. *Der Spiegel,* Issue 47, 1982.

64. Rudolf Bahro, *Pfeiler am anderen Ufer—Beiträge zur Politik der Grünen von Hagen bis Karlsruhe,* Berlin 1984, p. 21.

65. Ibid.

66. Petra Kelly, "Das System is bankrott—die neue Kraft muss her," in Petra Kelly and Jo Leinen (ed.), *Prinzip Leben, Die neue Kraft,* Berlin 1982, p. 137.

67. Ibid., pp. 136f.

68. *Bericht zur Lage der Fraktion,* op. cit., p. 67.

69. Petra K. Kelly, *Um Hoffnung kämpfen—Gewaltfrei in eine grüne Zukunft,* Bornheim/Merten 1983, pp. 167ff.

70. The survey was published in *Die Zeit,* January 11, 1985.

71. Donnella H. Meadows et al., *The Limits of Growth: A Report for the Club of Rome's Project on the Predicament of Mankind,* New York 1972.

72. Herbert Gruhl, *Ein Planet wird geplündert,* Frankfurt 1975.

73. Erhard Eppler, *Ende oder Wende,* Stuttgart-Berlin-Cologne-Mainz 1975.

74. Council on Environmental Quality, *The Global 2000 Report to the President,* Washington, D.C. 1980.

75. Cf. Ludwig Trepl, "Oekologie—eine grüne Leitwissenschaft?" in *Kursbuch 84,* December 1983, pp. 6ff.

76. *Das Bundesprogramm,* op. cit., p. 4.

77. Ibid.

78. Carl Amery, *Natur als Politik,* Reinbeck 1978, pp. 36ff.

79. Manon Maren Grisebach, *Philosophie der Grünen,* Munich-Vienna 1982, p. 32.

80. Ibid.

81. Ibid.

82. Wolf-Dieter and Conny Hasenclever, *Grüne Zeiten—Politik für eine lebenswerte Zukunft,* Munich 1983, p. 36 and p. 44.

83. Ibid., p. 44.

84. Peter Cornelius Mayer-Tasch, *Süddeutsche Zeitung,* March 26–27, 1983.

85. In this connection, see the argumentation by Kurt Sontheimer, *Zeitanwende? Die Bundesrepublik zwischen alter und alternativer Politik,* Hamburg 1983, p. 201.

86. See Hermann Schulte-Vennbur, "Wahrheitsokkupanten im neuen Gewand," in *Sonde,* Issue 4/84–1/85, pp. 16ff.

87. Fritjof Capra, *The Turning Point,* New York 1982, p. 412.

88. Grisebach, op. cit., p. 11.

89. *Der Spiegel,* September 20, 1982.

90. *Die Zeit,* July 9, 1982.

91. *Frankfurter Allgemeine Zeitung,* July 23, 1982.

92. Citation from Rupert Scholz, *Krise der parteienstaatlichen Demokratie?* Berlin–New York 1983; see also *Frankfurter Allgemeine Zeitung,* July 28, 1982.

93. Graue Zellen Westberlin, "Die Verkehrung des Subjects von der Klasse auf die Partei und autonome Bewegung," in Wolfgang Kraushaar (ed.), *Was sollen die Grünen im Parlament?* Frankfurt 1983, p. 52.

94. Bundesgeschäftsstelle der Grünen (ed.), *Gegen Arbeitslosigkeit und Sozialabbau ("Sindelfinger Programm"),* Bonn 1983, p. 32.

95. Die Grünen (ed.), *Das Bundesprogramm,* Bonn undated, p. 5.

96. Ibid.

97. See Robert Michels, *Zur Soziologie des Parteiwesens in der modernen Demokratie,* originally published 1911, 2d ed., Stuttgart 1970.

98. *Frankfurter Allgemeine Zeitung,* January 21, 1983.

99. Citation from *Frankfurter Allgemeine Zeitung,* July 2, 1983.

100. Rolf Dahrendorf, "Gefahr von der Basis," *Die Zeit,* April 15, 1983.

101. See Winfried Steffani, "Zur Vereinbarkeit von Basisdemokratie und parlamentarischer Demokratie," in *Aus Politik und Zeitgeschichte,* B2/83, January 15, 1983.

102. The dangers resulting from a dictatorship by the majority are correctly described in Friedbert Pflüger, "Die Grünen—Auf dem Weg in die 'totalitäre Demokratie'?" in *Sonde,* 1/1980, pp. 33ff.

103. *Der Spiegel,* Issue 24, June 13, 1983, p. 26.

104. Ibid., p. 25.

105. See page 5 of the minutes.

106. Parlamentskorrespondenz, *Heute im Bundestag,* June 8, 1983.

107. *Die Welt,* May 20, 1983; for a description as seen by the hecklers, see *radikal,* Issue 118/19, July-August 1983, p. 10.

108. *Frankfurter Allgemeine Zeitung,* February 10, 1982.

109. Ibid.

110. Ibid.

111. *Bericht zur Lage der Fraktion,* op. cit., pp. 18f.

112. For more details, see Langguth, *Protestbewegungen,* op. cit, pp. 263ff.

113. Geschäftsführender Ausschuss der Alternativen Liste für Demokratie und Umweltschutz (ed.), *Dokumentation über die Gewaltdiskussion in der Alternativen Liste Berlin,* Berlin undated.

114. *Der Spiegel,* Issue 24, June 13, 1983, p. 25.

115. Even writers, who should be particularly careful in the use of words, supported resistance by using the slogan "Defend Yourself!" A meeting of writers in December 1983 in Heilbronn called for a refusal of service in the armed forces. It was Günter Grass who drew the comparison with the resistance to National Socialism by stating: "I shall do those things which in the parlance of the immediate past were known as sedition (*Wehrkraftszersetzung*)."

116. For details, see Gerd Langguth, "Ziviler Ungehorsam—Weder legal noch legitim," in *Eichholzbrief,* Issue 3, 1984.

117. Johan Galtung, *Strukturelle Gewalt,* Reinbek bei Hamburg 1982, p. 9.

118. Theodor Ebert, *Sozialer Ungehorsam, Von der APO zur Friedensbewegung,* Waldkirch 1984, p. 271.

119. Sindelfinger Programm, op. cit., p. 6.

120. Ibid., p. 7.

121. Ibid.

122. Ibid., p. 19.

123. Cf. Frank Wolff and Eberhard Windaus, *Studentenbewegung 1967–1969,* Frankfurt 1977, pp. 219ff.

124. Interview in *Quick,* Issue 18, April 26, 1984.

125. Survey of the Institut für Demoskopie Allensbach, Ifd-Umfrage 4044, May 1984, published in *Allensbacher Berichte,* No. 16, June 1984.

126. *die tageszeitung,* May 7, 1984.

127. "Declaration on Peace," adopted by the Green Party at its Regular Federal Assembly, November 18–20, 1983, in Duisburg. For information on the Greens' foreign policy, all-German policy, and policy toward Europe, see the instructive analyses by Reinhard Stuth, "Die Aussen- und Deutschlandpolitik der Grünen," in Klaus Gotto and Hans-Joachim Veen (ed.), *die Grünen—Partei wider Willen,* Mainz 1984, pp. 54ff., and by the same author, "Europäische Fundamental-opposition," in *Sonde,* Issue 84/1–85, pp. 80ff.

128. *Bundesprogramm,* op. cit., p. 19.

129. Rudolf Bahro, "Wer zur Friedensbewegung steht," in *Grüner Basis-Dienst,* Issue 11, November 1983, pp. 31ff.

130. "Declaration on Peace," op. cit.

131. *Bundesprogramm,* op. cit., p. 19

132. For more information on the concept of social defense, see Bundesverband der Grünen (ed.), *Entrüstet Euch—Analysen zur atomaren Bedrohung—Wege zum Frieden,* Bonn undated.

133. *Grüner Basis-Dienst,* No. 1, January 1984, p. 18.

134. Zweites Deutsche Fernsehen, "Heute Journal," January 12, 1984.

135. *Frankfurter Allgemeine Zeitung,* November 3, 1983.

136. "Bericht zur Lage der Fraktion," op. cit., p. 84.

137. *Die Welt,* June 6, 1983.

138. Ernst Hoplitschek, one of the leaders of the Eco-Libertarians, stated: "In Baden-Württemberg or Bavaria, for example, I would build my strategy toward a coalition with the CDU or CSU. I don't see everything as falling under a conservative or reactionary heading" (*Stuttgarter Nachrichten,* February 25, 1984).

139. Joschka Fischer, "Für einen grünen Radikalreformismus," in Wolfgang Kraushaar, op. cit.

140. Citation from *Frankfurter Allgemeine Zeitung,* January 12, 1984.

141. The spokesman for the Greens' Federal Executive, Trampert, a representative of the so-called "Hamburg Line," apparently had a change of heart about possible cooperation with the SPD. When the results of the June 6, 1982, elections in Hamburg left the SPD in the

minority, he saw value in discussing possible cooperation. After the SPD regained a clear majority in the special elections of December 19, 1982, and was, therefore, no longer dependent on the GAL, he saw the identity of the Greens endangered. The Federal Executive and the Executive Committee of the Greens thereafter criticized the Hessen Greens and those Green members of the Bundestag who supported cooperation. In "today's economic power structure" and the "framework provided by the structure of society" a Green cabinet member would "be reduced to caricature," Trampert stated. (Citation from *Frankfurter Allgemeine Zeitung,* February 29, 1984.)

142. "Bericht zur Lage der Fraktion," op. cit., p. 76.

143. Zweites Deutsches Fernsehen, "Redaktionsbericht beim Deutschen Allgemeinen Sonntagsblatt," August 11, 1983.

144. Südfunk interview, November 27, 1983. This line was consistently restated by Schily in later interviews: "I am of the opinion that we should work toward cooperation with SPD, and that we should not exclude the possibility of becoming part of the Executive Branch" (Deutschlandfunk, February 8, 1984). In the SPD paper *Vorwärts,* he suggested to the Social Democrats that they join in a red-Green alliance. Such an alliance would lead to endurance tests inside the SPD and inside the Greens, but "if we take our own demands seriously, then I suggest that in spite of all its shortcomings, who other than the SPD would be our coalition partner?" The SPD leader in the Saarland, Oskar Lafontaine, would be an acceptable federal chancellor under such circumstances. In the long run, the Greens could not forever reject "the acceptance of responsibility in a coalition government" and should seek it (*Die Welt,* July 4, 1984).

145. Hessischer Rundfunk, February 26, 1984.

146. Wolfgang G. Gibowski, Forschungsgruppe Wahlen Mannheim, in "Bonner Perspektiven," Zweites Deutsches Fernsehen, January 22, 1984.

147. Werner A. Perger, "Die meisten Chancen hat die SPD als bessere CDU," in *Deutsches Allgemeines Sonntagsblatt,* September 23, 1984. This analysis is based on the surveys by the polling institutes Infratest and Sinus.

148. Statistisches Bundesamt (ed.), *Wahl zum 10. Deutschen Bundestag am 6. März 1983,* Volume 5: "Textliche Auswertung der Wahlergebnisse," Wiesbaden August 1984.

149. For the former role of the Young Socialists, see Gerd Langguth, "Jungsozialisten—Brückenkopf der APO in der SPD?" in *Sonde,* Issue 1, 1970, pp. 33ff.

150. *Die Welt,* February 21, 1984.

151. *Inner Sicherheit,* Bonn, Issue 48, May 18, 1979.

152. Printed in *Grüner Basis-Dienst,* Issue 1, January 1984, pp. 18f.

153. Lothar Bading, "Beispiel Hamburg, Soziale Bewegungen— Politische Strömungen und Verallgemeinerungen—Wahlen," in *Marxistische Studien und Forschungen (IMSF),* Issue 5, 1982, p. 124.

154. Parliamentary Undersecretary Carl-Dieter Spranger during the question period of the Bundestag on November 24, 1982.

155. Joachim Wagner, "Wer beeinflusst von linksaussen in Hamburg die Grünen?" in *Frankfurter Allgemeine Zeitung,* July 16, 1982.

156. *die tageszeitung,* August 10, 1982.

157. *Der Spiegel,* Issue 9, February 27, 1984.

158. See Ottheim Ramstedt, "Bewegung," in *Lexikon zur Soziologie,* Opladen 1973, p. 96.

159. Ibid.

160. "Bericht der Bundestagsfraktion der Grünen zur Bundesversammlung vom 7. bis 9. Dezember 1984 in Hamburg."

161. *Grüner Basis-Dienst,* Issue 1/1985, p. 46.

162. Joschka Fischer in *Der Spiegel,* Issue 9, February 27, 1984.

163. See especially the analysis by Günter Bannas, "Der Erfolg hält die Grünen zusammen," in *Frankfurter Allgemeine Zeitung,* June 6, 1984.

164. Social Science Research Institute (SFK) of the Konrad-Adenauer-Stiftung, Survey SFK 8401, 1984.

165. Social Science Research Institute of the Konrad-Adenauer-Stiftung.

166. See Langguth, "Jungsozialisten," op. cit., pp. 33ff.

167. *Der Spiegel,* Issue 22, May 28, 1984.

168. *Der Spiegel,* Issue 26, June 25, 1984.

169. Interview with Karl-Dietrich Bracher in "Report," October 23, 1984.

170. See Werner Weidenfeld, *Ratlose Normalität, Die Deutschen auf der Suche nach sich selbst,* Zurich 1984.

SUGGESTED READINGS

Rudolf Bahro, Die Alternative—Zur Kritik des real existierenden Sozialismus, Reinbek bei Hamburg 1980

Rudolf Bahro, Elemente einer neuen Politik, Berlin 1980

Rudolf Bahro, Pfeile am anderen Ufer, Berlin 1984

Rudolf Bahro, Wahnsinn mit Methode—Über die Logik der Blockkonfrontation, die Friedensbewegung, die Sowjetunion und die DKP, Berlin 1982

Wolfram Bickerich, (Hrsg.), SPD und Grüne—Das neue Bündnis? Reinbeck bei Hamburg 1985

Angeolo Bolaffi/Otto Kallscheuer, Die Grünen: Farbenlehre eines politischen Paradoxes, in: Probleme des Klassenkampfes, Heft 51 (13. Jahrgang 1983, Nr. 2), S. 62–105

Karl-Dietrich Bracher, Zeit der Ideologien—eine Geschichte politischen Denkens im 20. Jahrhundert, Stuttgart 1982

Rudolf Brun (Hrsg), Der grüne Protest—Herausforderung durch die Umweltparteien, Frankfurt 1978

Wilhelm P. Bürklin, Die Grünen und die Neue Politik, in: Politische Vierteljahresschrift (PVS), Heft 4, Dezember 1981

Wilhelm P. Bürklin, Grüne Politik—Ideologische Zyklen, Wähler und Parteiensystem, Opladen 1984

Fritjof Capra, The Tao of Physics, Berkeley, California 1975

Fritjof Capra, The Turning Point, New York 1982

Fritjof Capra/Charlene Spretnak, Green Politics—The Global Promise, New York 1984

Carl Doggs, "The Greens, Anti-Militarism and the Global Crisis," in Radical America, Boston, Vol. 17, No. 1, 1983

Dieter Duhm, Aufbruch zur neuen Kultur, München 1984

Thomas Ebermann/Rainer Trampert, Die Zukunft der Grünen—Ein realistisches Konzept für eine radikale Partei, Hamburg 1984

John Ely, "The Greens: Ecology and the Promise of Radical Democracy," in Radical America, Boston, Vol. 17, No. 1, 1983

Joschka Fischer, Von grüner Kraft und Herrlichkeit, Reinbeck bei Hamburg 1984

Helmut Fogt, Basisdemokratie oder Herrschaft der Aktivisten? Zum Politikverständnis der Grünen, in: Politische Vierteljahresschrift (PVS), Heft 1, 1984, Seite 97–114

Helmut Fogt, Die Grünen in den Parlamenten der Bundersrepublik. Ein Soziogramm, in: Zeitschrift für Parlamentsfragen, Heft 4, Dezember 1983, S. 500–517

Freibeuter, Das grüne Ei, Nr. 15, Berlin 1983

Herbert Gruhl, Ein Planet wird geplündert, Frankfurt 1975

Wolf-Dieter Hasenclever, Die Grünen und die Bürger—ein neues Selbstverständnis als politische Partei?, in: Joachim Raschke (Hrsg.), Bürger und Parteien, Bonn 1982

Wolf-Dieter und Connie Hasenclever, Grüne Zeiten—Politik für eine lebenswerte Zukunft, München 1982

Gerhard Herdegen, Die neue Farbe, in: Die politische Meinung, 25/ 1980, S. 17–25

Joseph Huber, Basisdemokratie und Parlamentarismus, in: Aus Politik und Zeitgeschichte, B 2/15. Januar 1983

Joseph Huber, Wer soll das alles ändern?—Die Alternativen der Alternativbewegung, Berlin 1981

Brigitte Jäger/Claudia Pinl, Zwischen Rotation und Routine—die Grünen im Bundestag, Köln 1985

Petra K. Kelly, Um Hoffnung kämpfen—Gewaltfrei in eine grüne Zukunft, Bornheim-Merten 1983

Petra K. Kelly/Jo Leinen (Hrsg.), Prinzip Leben—Ökopax—Die neue Kraft, Berlin 1982

Thomas Kluge (ed.), Grüne Politik—der Stand einer Auseinandersetzung, Frankfurt 1984

Wolfgang Kraushaar (Hrsg.), Was sollen die Grünen im Parlament? Frankfurt 1983

Kursbuch—Zumutungen an die Grünen, Dezember 1983

Gerd Langguth, Bundeswehr, NATO, Freundschaft mit den USA: In der jungen Generation nicht mehr gefragt?, in: Politische Studien, Heft 272, November/Dezember 1983

Gerd Langguth, Jugend ist anders—Portrait einer jungen Generation, Freiburg-Basel-Wien 1983

Gerd Langguth, Protestbewegung, Entwicklung—Niedergang—Renaissance, Köln 1983

Hans-Werner Lüdke/Olaf Dinné, Die Grünen, Personen—Projekte, Programme, Stuttgart 1980

Manon Maren-Grisebach, Philosophie der Grünen, München 1982

Jörg R. Mettke (Hrsg.), Die Grünen—Regierungspartner von morgen? Reinbek bei Hamburg 1982

Rolf Meyer/Günter Handlögten, Die Grünen vor der Wahl, in: Aus Parlament und Zeitgeschichte, B 36/6. September 1980

Emil-Peter Müller, Die Grünen und das Parteiensystem, Köln 1984

Detlef Murphy, Grüne und Bunte—Theorie und Praxis, "alternativer Parteien," in: Joachim Raschke (Hrsg.), Bürger und Parteien, Bonn 1982

Heinrich Oberreuter, Abgesang auf einen Verfassungstyp?, in: Aus Politik und Zeitgeschichte, B 2/15. Januar 1983

Robert L. Pfalzgraff, Jr./Kim R. Holmes/Clay Clemens/Werner Kaltefleiter, The Greens of West Germany, Cambridge, Massachusetts and Washington, D.C. 1983

Friedbert Pflüger, Die Grünen—auf dem Weg in die "totalitäre Demokratie?", in: Sonde 1/1980, S. 24–39

Jonathon Porritt, Seeing Green—The Politics of Ecology Explained, Oxford 1984

Winfried Schlaffke, Abseits, Die Alternativen—Irrweg oder neue Weltkultur? Köln 1979

Rupert Scholz, Krise der parteienstaatlichen Demokratie? in: Schriftenreihe der Juristischen Gesellschaft e. V., Berlin, Heft 80

Ernst Friedrich Schumacher, Small is Beautiful—A Study of Economics as if People Mattered, London 1974

Kurt Sontheimer, Zeitwende? Die Bundesrepublik Deutschland zwischen alter und alternativer Politik, Hamburg 1983

Winfried Steffani, Zur Vereinbarkeit von Basisdemokratie und parlamentarischer Demokratie, in: Aus Politik und Zeitgeschichte, B 2/15. Januar 1983

Erwin Teufel, Die Grünen zwischen Bewegung und Partei, in: Sonde, Nr. 3/82

Klaus G. Troitzsch, Die Herausforderung der "etablierten" Parteien durch die "Grünen," in: Heino Kaack/Reinhold Roth (Hrsg.), Handbuch des deutschen Parteiensystems, Opladen 1980, S. 260–294

Hans-Joachim Veen, Wer wählt grün?; in: Aus Politik und Zeitgeschichte, B 35–36/84, 1.9.

Antje Vollmer, . . . und wehret euch täglich!, Bonn—ein Grünes Tagebuch, Gütersloh 1984

Bodo Zeuner, Aktuelle Anmerkungen zum Postulat der "Basisdemokratie" bei den Grünen/Alternativen, in: Probleme des Klassenkampfs, Heft 51 (13. Jahrgang 1983, Nr. 2), S. 106–117

ORGANIZATIONS

Action Association of Independent Germans/(AUD) Aktion
Unabhängiger Deutscher
Alternative List/(AL) Alternative Liste
Alternative List for Democracy and Environmental
Protection, Berlin/(AL) Alternative Liste für Demokratie &
Umweltschutz, Berlin
Alternative List in Bremen/Alternative Bremen
Christian Democratic Union/Christian Social Union
(Bavarian Wing of the Party)/Christlich-Demokratische
Union (CDU)/Christlich Soziale Union (CSU)
Communist Association/(KB) Kommunistischer Bund
Communist Association of West Germany/(KBW)
Kommunisticher Bund Westdeutschland
Communist Party of Germany/(KPD) Kommunistische Partei
Deutschlands
Democratic Ecological Party/(OeDP) Oekologisch-
Demokratische Partei
Federal Association of Citizen Initiatives for the Protection
of the Environment/(BBU) Bundesverband Bürgerinitiativen
& Umweltschutz
Federal party committee (BHA)
Free Democratic Party/(FDP) Frei Demokratische Partei
German Communist Party/(DKP) Deutsche Kommunistische
Partei

German Trade Union Federation/Deutscher
　　Gewerkschaftsbund
Gray Cells of Berlin/Graue Zellen Westberlin
Green Action for the Future/(GAZ) Grüne Aktion Zukunft
Green-Alternative List in Hamburg/(GAL) Grün-Alternative
　　Liste Hamburg
Green List for the Protection of the Environment/(GLU)
　　Grüne Liste Umweltschutz
Green List for the Protection of the Environment in Hessen/
　　Grüne Liste Umweltschutz, Hessen
Green List in Bremen/Bremer Grüne Liste
Green List in Hessen/Grüne Liste Hessen
Independent Socialdemocratic Party of Germany/(USPD)
　　Unabhänginge Sozialdemokratische Partei Deutschlands
Institute for Marxist Studies and Research (IMSR)
List for Democracy and Protection of the Environment/Liste
　　für Demokratie und Umweltschutz
Marxist Student Association/(MSB) Marxistischer
　　Studentenbund Spartakus
North Atlantic Treaty Organization (NATO)
Other Political Associations–The Greens/(SPV–the Greens)
　　Sonstige Politische Vereinigung–Die Grünen
Red Army Faction/Rote Armee-Fraktion
Social Democratic Party of Germany/(SPD)
　　Sozialdemokratische Partei Deutschlands
Socialist Bureau/(SB) Sozialistisches Büro
Socialist German Workers Youth/(SDAJ) Sozialistiche
　　Deutsche Arbeiterjugend
Socialist Initiative/Sozialistische Initiative
Socialist Student Association/(SDS) Sozialistischer Deutscher
　　Studentenbund
Young Pioneers/(JP) Junge Pioniere
Young Socialists/Jungsozialisten
Z-Group/Gruppe Z

INDEX OF PERSONAL NAMES